APPLES to CIDER

APPLES to CIDER

How to make cider at home

APRIL WHITE *with* STEPHEN WOOD *of Farnum Hill Ciders*

WITHDRAWN

Quarry Books
100 Cummings Center, Suite 406L
Beverly, MA 01915

quarrybooks.com • quarryspoon.com

© 2015 by Quarry Books

First published in the United States of America in 2015 by
Quarry Books, a member of
Quarto Publishing Group USA Inc.
100 Cummings Center
Suite 406-L
Beverly, Massachusetts 01915-6101
Telephone: (978) 282-9590
Fax: (978) 283-2742
www.quarrybooks.com
Visit www.QuarrySPOON.com and help us celebrate food and culture one spoonful at a time!

10 9 8 7 6 5 4 3 2 1

ISBN: 978-1-59253-918-5

Digital edition published in 2015
eISBN: 978-1-62788-315-6

Library of Congress Cataloging-in-Publication Data available

Cover and Book Design: Laura McFadden
Page Layout: *tabula rasa* graphic design

Printed in China

In memory of Terry Maloney of West County Cider, Colrain, Massachusetts

CONTENTS

Introduction

Cider is nothing more than apples, fermented. It seems simple, until you taste the end result of the fermentation. Good cider, like good wine, starts with good fruit. The fermentation process brings forward the hidden aromas, tastes, and sensations of those apples. When blended and fermented, the most celebrated cider apples—often called inedible—reveal flavors such as apricot, black tea, honey, and pine. These flavors balanced with acidity, astringency, and bitterness, create a combination that has made cider a popular drink for centuries.

Cidermaking, too, seems simple. The basic process is straightforward. It requires minimal ingredients and equipment, most readily available from home wine or brewing supply shops. It requires minimal space, making it a manageable at-home project. But good cidermaking also requires patience, persistence, and practice.

The crew behind Poverty Lane Orchards and Farnum Hill Ciders has been making still and sparkling ciders for two decades. It is a learning process, even after hundreds of batches. In that time, they have also watched the apple and cider industries change, and an interest in well-made cider and home cidermaking grow. In this book, they share their years of experience and the philosophy of cidermaking they have developed: For these cidermakers, the cidermaking process begins with the apple.

THE FARNUM HILL CIDERS STORY

The seeds of Farnum Hill Ciders were sown in the 1960s, when Poverty Lane Orchards was planted on the site of a former dairy farm. Its northern New Hampshire hills were planted with McIntosh and Cortland, then two of the leading varieties of wholesale apples. Stephen Wood was introduced to apple farming in 1965. He was eleven years old when his father and a partner purchased the farm. No one was thinking about cidermaking at Poverty Lane Orchards then, at least not beyond the occasional barrel of New England–style cider fermenting haphazardly over the winter.

Few people were thinking about cidermaking anywhere at the time. The popularity of cider in the United States had waned with Prohibition almost five decades earlier, and taste for cider in traditional cidermaking regions throughout Europe was declining, too.

When Wood began to manage the farm in the late 1970s the focus was still on packing classic New England apples for sale throughout the region, but the apple industry was changing rapidly. Imported fruit began to arrive—shiny Red Delicious apples from the West Coast and tart Granny Smiths from South America—reducing demand for Cortlands and McIntosh. Wood needed a way to distinguish Poverty Lane Orchards in the now-crowded apple market. In thinking about the future of the orchard, he looked to the past, to many nearly forgotten varieties of heirloom eating apples and to the inedible varieties traditional in Europe's main cider apple-growing regions. Those inedible apples were part of the continent's long cidermaking tradition.

In travels through England in the 1980s, Wood met the cidermakers behind many of the country's storied ciders and learned from them. He began experimenting with growing traditional European cider apples in New England, at first dedicating just 5 acres (2 ha) of the then-90-acre (36 ha) orchard to the unheard of idea of modern American cider, and he began experimenting with cidermaking techniques. Some of that early cider was tasty. Some was terrible. But by the mid-1990s, Poverty Lane Orchards was turning those inedible European apples with obscure names such as Dabinett, Medaille d'Or, Kingston Black, and Stoke Red into delicious Farnum Hill Ciders.

THE FARNUM HILL CIDERS PHILOSOPHY

For Wood, cidermaker Nicole LeGrand Leibon, and the rest of the crew behind Farnum Hill Ciders, cider is all about the apple. A cidermaker's responsibility is to coax the best from the fruit without unnecessary additives or techniques that would obscure the apple. The Farnum Hill Ciders still cidermaking process, outlined in chapter 5, is a largely hands-off one. A cidermaker's main task is to find the best apple juice available and provide good conditions for fermentation to occur.

Finding high-quality apple juice for cidermaking has long been a challenge, but as more people become cidermakers—commercial or hobbyist—more orchards are cultivating cider apples to meet the demand.

As interest in cidermaking and, even more importantly, cider drinking has increased, Poverty Lane Orchards has found like-minded commercial and home cidermakers in diverse apple-growing regions. Cidermakers such as E.Z. Orchards, Eve's Cidery, and Eden Orchards share the Farnum Hill Ciders philosophy, while making very different ciders. (Their cidermaking processes for *cidre*, *méthode champenoise*, and ice cider are outlined in chapter 7.)

A Note for the Home Brewer

The process of making cider is most similar to the process of making wine. For the home brewer used to making beer, this can be a shock. There's simply less to do and fewer opportunities to affect the final product. Cidermaking is an exercise in patience. Cider does not benefit from frequent attention. Instead, cider is best when left alone for much of the fermentation process. And cider doesn't benefit from unnecessary additives that hide the natural flavors of the apple. Cider, like wine, is an agricultural product and each batch you make will be unique.

CHAPTER

What Is Cider?

What is cider? In the United States, that's a harder question than you might think.

In American English, cider can be, simply, the juice pressed from an apple. This fresh, sweet liquid is bottled and sold as sweet cider, a staple of the New England fall. But the word *cider* can also refer to something more complex—the juice pressed from an apple and turned, through the magic known as fermentation, into a delicious, alcoholic hard cider.

Elsewhere in the world, particularly in regions with strong cider-making traditions, there is little confusion between sweet cider and hard cider—or *cidre* or *sidra*, as it is known in France and Spain, respectively—but there can be much disagreement about what makes for the best cider.

CIDER HISTORY

Hard cider can trace its history back two millennia. Interest in the apple goes back even further. Wild apples are depicted in cave art from before 8000 BCE.

It is believed that the species of apple that has become one of the most widely cultivated crops on the planet comes from the Tian Shan Mountains of what is now Kazakhstan. Trade routes between the Mediterranean and the Far East are credited with spreading the fruit. And with the apple came cider. Cider was practical, a way to use and preserve excess apples from the harvest. Although the science was not understood, cider was also a safe alternative to water, which often carried diseases. Cider's alcohol level was high enough to make it inhospitable to many bacteria, but low enough that even children drank cider. Although much of early cidermaking is lost to history, there are references to cider as early as 55 BCE. By the eighth-century reign of Charlemagne, whose empire encompassed much of Europe's top apple producing regions including Northern Spain, cider (or *poatum*, as it was known) was produced on royal estates.

Modern cidermaking dates back mere centuries to the apple orchards and farms of Northern France and Southern England. By the late-sixteenth century, the Normans were cultivating varieties of cider apples that cidermakers still talk about today. In the seventeenth century, the cider tradition took firm root in England. And, as explorers set out from England, Spain, and France for the new world, they took with them both apple seeds and grafting wood, which grew especially well in the English colonies on the East Coast of North America, and an interest in cider.

Cider became commonplace in the colonies and stories abound of widespread production, copious consumption—President John Adams is said to have drunk cider every morning, for his well-being—and even of its use as currency.

Throughout its history, the popularity of cider waxed and waned for numerous reasons. Cider production and consumption rose and fell with changes in growing conditions, taxation policies, immigration patterns, social movements and, simply, tastes. In America, the temperance movement of the nineteenth and early twentieth century halted cider's rise—and introduced sweet, unfermented, cider into the lexicon.

What Is Perry?

When pears are milled and pressed and the juice is fermented, the resulting alcoholic beverage is known as perry. Though delicious, pears and perry have never enjoyed the widespread popularity of apples and cider.

Like the apples used to make cider, pears cultivated for perry are typically high in both sugars and tannins, with an astringency that makes them unpopular for eating out of hand. The perry-making process is similar to the cidermaking process. If you have access to the juice from perry pears, experiment with the cidermaking process outlined in chapter 5.

CIDER SCIENCE

The cidermaking process, described in extensive detail in this book, is designed to promote alcoholic fermentation. It is similar to the process for turning grapes into wine. There are innumerable variables in cidermaking—including the tastes of the cidermaker—and many different styles, but the basic steps are the same.

Cidermaking begins with ripe apples, which have a high concentration of sugar. The sugar is the food for the yeast, which will convert it into alcohol and carbon dioxide. A cidermaker's choice of apples has the biggest impact on the cider produced. Most cider is made from a blend of apples, which are then pressed into juice. The cidermaker is looking for a balance of sensations and flavors, paying attention to the acids and tannins of the cider apples. The cidermaker may choose to blend the juices again after fermentation (see chapter 7). The result of blending at each stage is different, something that the cidermaker learns through experimentation and experience.

The chosen apples are milled into a pulp, called pomace, and then pressed to extract the juice. (Most home cidermakers will begin the cidermaking process with juice.) The juice is then fermented.

There are many styles of cider. In some the juice is fermented spontaneously, relying on the existing yeast. In other styles—often preferred by home cidermakers for their reliability—the juice is inoculated with specifically selected yeasts. Cidermaking is mostly a hands-off process; the yeast, not the cidermaker, must do the work, but cidermakers try to influence the fermentation process by controlling the nutrients available in the juice or by adjusting the temperature. Typically, a long, slow fermentation is the goal.

Depending on the style of cider being produced and the preferences of the cidermaker, the cider may be bottled before the fermentation process is complete, immediately after the process is complete, or after a maturation period.

Fermentation tanks filled with cider

CIDER STYLES

The topic of cider styles is much debated among today's cidermakers, who will often use the word traditional to describe their ciders. As with wine, easy categorization of an agricultural product made in different geographic regions, with different varieties of fruit, by different techniques, for different tastes, over thousands and thousands of years is impossible.

For the home cidermaker, a discussion of cider styles is important not to establish strict definitions or anoint one approach as the best, but to provide a basic understanding of common, often overlapping, vocabulary. Styles defined by geography, method of production, and taste profiles will come up frequently in conversations with fellow cidermakers and on the back labels of cider bottles.

Geography

A geographic style develops over decades, or perhaps centuries, as cidermakers in a specific region, working with similar types of apples grown in similar conditions learn from and influence each other. Over time, one approach to cidermaking becomes the standard against which the region's cider drinkers compare all other ciders. When enough time has passed, the style is often described as "authentic" or "traditional," although by that time, few people in the region may still be making cider in that method.

To categorize styles by region, one must use a broad brush. Not all ciders produced in a given region will adhere to the style, and even ciders that do adhere to geographic style will not share every characteristic. The particular source of the fruit or the cidermaker's own preferences will influence the cider. Further, a general geographic style may sometimes be broken down into more specific regional styles, though these distinctions are far more useful when studying the history of cider than when producing it or drinking it today.

Cider is made in apple-growing regions around the world, such as Germany, Finland, and South Africa, but the most widely recognized styles have emerged from the most established cider-producing countries: England, France, and Spain. Although relatively new to the cidermaking scene, Quebec has also developed a distinctive style of ice cider.

England

The United Kingdom produces nearly half of the world's cider. Its cidermaking roots are in the west and southwest of England. Many cidermakers speak of the counties of Herefordshire, Gloucestershire, Worcestershire, Somerset, and Devon with reverence. Historically, the ciders made in the region were based on the local bittersweet apples, with strong tannins as well as noticeable acid. They were fermented to full dryness, and most often they were still, not sparkling, beverages best served in a pint glass.

Most widely available commercial brands today describe themselves as English-style ciders. Many are still or somewhat fizzy, comparable to the carbonation of a beer, and best served in a pint glass, but most have more sweetness and less of the tannins traditionally associated with the region. The term *farmhouse cider* is frequently heard in reference to English-style ciders. The term originally described the small-batch ciders produced by local farmers. These ciders were typically still and strongly tannic. Today, the term is widely used to give cider drinkers an impression that their cider is natural and straight from the orchard, whether that is a true reflection of the process or not.

Traditional English-style cider is made through a process similar to the one described in chapter 5.

France

France is well known for natural *cidre* with low alcohol, residual sweetness, fruity flavors, and some sparkle. In the traditional cidermaking region of Normandy—and specifically in Pays d'Auge—the amber-hued cider tends to be sweeter with a head of fine bubbles. In the country's other traditional cidermaking region of Brittany, the clearer cider tends to be drier and is served in a *bolée*, which resembles a teacup.

The style developed, in part, from the apples commonly grown in the region: high-tannin, low-acid bittersweets. Many French ciders are made using the wild yeasts present on the apples. A process called *keeving* is responsible for the sweetness and fruity flavors and aromas for many classic French ciders. In the keeving process, the fresh juice is stripped of nitrogen and other nutrients that yeast need in addition to sugar to thrive. The undernourished yeast ferment the juice very slowly, without the production of undesirable gases, and die off before converting all the juice's sugars to alcohol, producing a clear, sweeter cider.

For the home cidermaker, this approach to cidermaking can be difficult; undernourished yeasts are also a cause of many cider flaws, and unpleasant flavors and aromas.

The sparkle in traditional French cider often comes from completing fermentation in the bottle. However, because *méthode champenoise* has its roots in the Champagne region of France, ciders produced by this method are sometimes associated with the country.

Spain

The Asturias and Basque regions of Spain are home to the country's "authentic" cider production. In Spanish, the beverage is *sidra natural*; in the Basque language, it is *sagardoa*. The ciders, made primarily with sharp apples and wild yeasts, are traditionally similar: dry with a solid tannic structure and a very slight effervescence, served young. A high level of volatile acidity can give the ciders a vinegar-like bite that sets them apart from those produced in other geographic traditions. Because the ciders are not filtered, the liquid is hazy.

There is also tradition in the consumption of Spanish ciders. Cider is not poured from a bottle into a glass, but "thrown." The cider is poured just a mouthful at a time from a height into a tilted glass, hitting the side of the glass before collecting in the bottom. The splashy pour aerates and lightly carbonates the liquid, though the results last for only a minute or two. The cider drinker is meant to down the cider quickly, tossing any collected sediment, before asking for another.

Quebec

Cider has been made throughout Quebec, and indeed, in many places in Canada, for centuries, but its unique ice cider—or *cidre de glace*—style emerged only a few decades ago. Like the traditional cider styles that developed in Europe, Quebec's style is peculiar to its geography. The ice-cidermaking process takes advantage of the region's frigid winters. Through the natural cycle of freezing and thawing, the sugars in the apple juice (or, on rare occasion, in the apples themselves) are concentrated before fermentation. The finished ice cider is a full-bodied after-dinner drink with an 8 to 12 percent alcohol. The style is also popular in neighboring northern New England and Northern New York, which shares Quebec's climate.

CIDER METHODS

Although certain methods of cider-making are often associated with certain cidermaking regions, their use is not strictly limited by geography. Because these methods can produce different results when used with different fruit from different regions, it can be instructive to discuss method apart from geography. The main distinction between the methods discussed here is when fermentation is completed: before bottling, in-bottle, or before bottling with a second fermentation in bottle.

Full alcoholic fermentation before bottling

A cider that is fully fermented before bottling will still be cider (unless carbon dioxide is later added; see chapter 7). Almost all ciders that are fermented fully before bottling are fermented to dryness; that is, there are no residual sugars present in the cider. This method is common in traditional English cidermaking. It is the method used to make Farnum Hill Ciders and outlined in chapter 5.

Alcoholic fermentation finished in bottle

When cider is bottled before fermentation is complete, the cider develops a natural carbonation from the carbon dioxide produced by the continuing fermentation. This approach is common in French-style cidermaking. These ciders are fermented slowly, often using wild yeast, and can be bottled as a semi-sweet or dry cider. In the bottle it will develop fine, integrated bubbles, which may be considered preferable to the larger bubbles produced by adding carbonation after fermentation. This is the method used by E.Z. Orchards and outlined in chapter 7.

Second alcoholic fermentation in bottle

Méthode champenoise relies on a second alcoholic fermentation that takes place in the bottle. The process begins after a cider has undergone a full alcoholic fermentation before bottling. The dry cider is then inoculated with additional yeast and sugar before bottling. The yeast and sugar undergo a fermentation that creates fine bubbles in the bottled cider as well as some of the yeasty character-istics often associated with Champagne. This is the method used by Eve's Cidery and outlined in chapter 7.

The term *secondary fermentation* can also be used to refer to malolactic fermentation. This is different from alcoholic fermentation. In malolactic fermentation, malic acid is converted into lactic acid. This leaves the cider without noticeable acid and is considered a flaw by some. (See chapter 6.)

CIDER TASTES

For the typical home cidermaker, the most apparent distinctions between ciders are the aromas, tastes, and sensations experienced when drinking the cider. These characteristics are the result of the apples and method used to produce the cider, but they are another way to divide the world of cider into categories for discussion and debate.

Still versus sparkling

Still cider, as classically produced in England, is less common among today's cider offerings. More often you'll encounter ciders that range from slightly effervescent (similar to a typical draft beer) to sparkling (like a Champagne). As discussed, any still cider can be carbonated, producing larger bubbles, or a cidermaker can produce smaller bubbles though in-bottle or post-bottling fermentation. Some of Farnum Hill Ciders are still, while others are carbonated after fermentation.

Acid levels

The apples used in the cidermaking process are key in determining how much acid will be present in the finished cider. However, some geographic styles favor acid (England, Spain) while others (France) disfavor it. Likewise, some methods preserve the juice's acid, while others encourage mellow acid or even malolactic fermentation.

Tannic structure

As with acid, tannic structure is determined largely by the apples used. The bittersweet cider apples grown in the English countryside typically contribute strong tannins to ciders. The same is true for cider made from bittersweet apples through most cidermaking methods.

Residual and returned sugars

Semi-sweet ciders are made by halting the fermentation before the yeasts convert all of the sugars present to alcohol. Geographically, sweeter ciders are common in France, where the keeving method stops the fermentation. Finishing fermentation in the bottle also allows for the production of semi-sweet ciders. Some ciders, particularly mass-market ciders, are sweetened after fermentation like most champagnes.

OTHER TERMS

There are countless other ways to describe and categorize cider, some more useful than others. Home cidermakers will also encounter many other alcoholic beverages produced from apples.

Apple brandy: A spirit distilled from cider, also known as Calvados (which correctly refers to apple brandy produced in the Calvados section of France). Apple brandy is distilled twice to 70 to 75 percent alcohol and barrel-aged.

Applejack: Another name for apple brandy, or a moonshine produced by freezing and thawing hard cider to concentrate the alcohol.

Apple wine: A fruit wine, in which sugar is added to apple juice before fermentation to increase the final alcohol level.

Cyser: A mead-like drink in which honey is added to apple juice before fermentation.

Flavored cider: A drink in which apple juice is fermented with the juice of another fruit. In commercial production, flavored ciders are often flavored with additional fruit after fermentation.

"New England" cider: A 7 to 13 percent alcohol drink, in which sugar, molasses, or maple syrup is added to apple juice before fermentation to increase the final alcohol level. Raisins are often also added. "New England" cider is uncommon in modern cider production.

Pommeau: A blend of apple brandy and sweet cider, aged in oak. About 16 to 18 percent alcohol.

CIDER TRENDS

Over the past fifty years there have been two dominant trends in commercial cidermaking. One is the rise of large companies producing cider for the mass market; the other is the growth in small-batch commercial production (as well, of course, as an increasing number of home cidermakers).

Most mass-market ciders pay homage to the traditions of English cidermaking in their marketing. The majority of these ciders—increasingly found on tap or in the supermarket's beer section—have the slight fizz sometimes associated with commercial English ciders. However, these modern ciders are often sweeter and fruitier than typical of the category, with less of the style's bittersweet characteristics.

The small-batch producers whose ciders are becoming more available, particularly in the United States, are even more difficult to categorize. The largest growth of cideries in recent years has occurred in the larger apple-growing regions: the Northeast (particularly northern New England and New York), the Mid-Atlantic (dominated by Virginia), the Northwest, and Michigan.

As the modern cidermaking culture in these regions is relatively new, no distinct geographic style has developed yet. Instead, these small-batch producers are experimenting with many different methods of cidermaking and adapting old geographic traditions to different apple varieties, new technologies, and current tastes.

Home cidermakers have this same opportunity: to learn from cider's history and then use those lessons to make a cider they love with the ingredients and equipment available.

The Farnum Hill Ciders "Style"

By good luck alone, in the early 1980s, I got to know several apple growers in Hereford and Somerset (two of the chief cider counties of England) and spent a fair amount of time in their orchards, cider rooms, and homes.

We grew curious here at Poverty Lane Orchards. Our New Hampshire climates and soils are very different from those of the west of England. Could New Hampshire grow any of the extraordinary cider apples common across the ocean? We began experimenting by grafting hundreds of cider and heirloom varieties to old settled trees. We planted our first cider orchard in 1989—still something of an experiment. It was meant to be our only cider orchard. We had no idea what we were about to do.

But, during that same time, apple market conditions were changing. We began to doubt the future profitability of medium-sized wholesale New England orchards like ours. Within a few years, we knew we had to change as well or give up growing apples. By then, we had a decade of horticultural experience with cider apple varieties. On the strength of that meager experience—together with curiosity and slight desperation—we pulled out many acres of productive McIntosh, Cortland, and other market apple varieties, and replanted them with inedible cider fruit.

It's a good thing that apple trees take some time to actually bear crops, because it took us a fair long time to learn to make cider that was even drinkable, let alone good. At first, we hoped to make an English-style cider and a French-style cider. But by the late 1990s, we were regularly finding aromas and flavors in our ciders that we'd never encountered in England or France. One happy day, we suddenly asked one another why we'd been trying to make imitative ciders instead of trying to just make something delicious and reflective of our apples and our land. This is the USA, after all. On that day, the Farnum Hill Ciders style (if there is such a thing) was born.

We've learned a bit about cidermaking since those days. We've changed a few of the cider varieties we grow and use, and a few of our practices in the cider room. But the principles haven't wavered. We want our cider to have a good tannic structure, plenty of fruit, a faint earthy background, and a nice bright acidity (especially at the end). We want to bring the character of our orchards, and the fruit we grow here, to the bottle as handsomely as possible. And we want never to complacently believe that we know exactly how to do it. Our ciders and orchards will continue to improve for as long as we remember how little we understand about apples, land, and cider—and how much we have yet to learn.

sting Cider

...ider is an important part of cidermaking.

...earn the most from your cider tasting if you develop a
...e and a vocabulary for tasting that controls as many
...s possible and allows for consistent and objective evalua-
...n batch of cider. The process in this chapter was devel-
...many years by the Farnum Hill Ciders crew.

...ns with the apples, happens again when the apples are
...' pressed, when the fermentation is completed, when
...acked, when the fermented batches are blended, and as
the cider matures. The apples and the juice are very different from
the fermented cider, showing fewer nuances and different flavors.
The crew regularly tastes other people's cider, which they refer to as
OPC, to learn from other cidermakers.

During the tasting process, the cidermakers do not pass judgment on a cider. That comes later when they make decisions about what to blend and sell. During the tasting process, they are intent only on describing it. And the descriptions they use to do so—be it "honey" and "sweet cream" or "forest floor" and "barnyard"—are viewed as neither positive nor negative.

It takes some practice to become comfortable with applying an objective standard of evaluation to the fundamentally subjective topics of smell and taste. But this process is as indispensable to the home cidermaker as it is to commercial cidermakers.

You should plan to taste lots of cider to train your senses and begin to understand the different types of cider available. You should also plan to taste the apple juice before you begin the fermentation process and to taste the cider when fermentation is complete. If you plan to let the cider sit on the lees or to mature before bottling, you may choose to taste the cider at other times in the cidermaking process. (Learn more about these topics in chapter 5.)

It takes a lot of practice, too, not to let the tasting process affect your enjoyment of cider. When you are conducting a tasting, do so carefully and analytically. When you pour a cider after work, just drink it.

PREPARING FOR A TASTING

When preparing for a tasting, it is important to control as many variables of the experience as possible. You are looking for changes in the juice and cider over time, so you want to ensure that the changes you perceive in the glass are not a result of changes in the environment.

Where to Taste

If possible, taste in a room that is free of noticeable aromas. (For instance, tasting in the kitchen while dinner is cooking is not the best choice.) Similarly, you don't want to be wearing strong perfumes or using strongly scented soap during the tasting. And don't taste with food, which will change your perception of smell, taste, and sensation.

Equipment

You will need some easy-to-find equipment for the tasting: cider; plastic tubing; a clean pitcher for cider; dry cider, neutral white wine, or distilled water, as needed to top off the fermentation container; a bucket filled with warm water; a thermometer; clean tasting glasses; a spit bucket; and a notebook.

Using the same style of glasses for each tasting is another way of controlling external variables. The style of glass will affect your perceptions. A overly narrow glass, such as a Champagne flute, leaves little room for your nose, decreasing your access to the aromas, while an overly wide glass, such as a white wine glass, allows the more volatile aromas to dissipate quickly. The best glasses for tasting juice and cider are standard wine-tasting glasses, which have a wide cup that narrows toward the opening. The wide cup allows you to easily swirl the liquid and release aromas, and the narrower opening funnels the aromas while leaving room for your nose.

You will also want to use the same notebook for each tasting. You'll want to compare your notes to learn more about your cider and your senses. For the same reason, it's also ideal to taste with the same people each time.

Collect all the equipment you need before beginning the tasting.

CIDERMAKING TIP

Equipment for Tasting

Collect the following equipment before beginning a tasting.

- Cider
- Plastic tubing
- Clean pitchers for juice or cider
- Dry cider, neutral white wine, or distilled water, as needed to top off the carboy
- Bucket filled with warm water
- Thermometer
- Clean wine-tasting glasses
- Spit bucket
- Notebook

PREPARING THE CIDER

The plastic tubing will be used to siphon some cider into the pitcher. You want about 2 ounces (60 ml) of cider per taster. If you take too much cider from a carboy, you will have to use more dry cider, neutral white wine, or distilled water to replace it. If you take too little cider, you won't be able to fully evaluate it.

If you are tasting cider that has finished fermenting, it's important to replace the removed cider with another liquid to fill the carboy completely and minimize exposure to air. Add dry cider, neutral white wine, or distilled water before resealing the carboy.

If you are tasting bottled cider, you can pour the cider directly into the pitcher. Although you could skip the pitcher and pour directly from the bottle, tasters can be influenced by what they expect a cider to taste like; it's best to remove visual clues, such as a distinctive bottle or label. Tasting blind removes another variable from the experience.

Place the pitcher or pitchers of cider in the bucket filled with warm water. The water bath will bring the cider to a proper tasting temperature more quickly, which means the cider will spend less time exposed to air, which can change its properties. The ideal tasting temperature is about 60°F (16°C), which might be slightly warmer than you would typically serve your cider. At or just above 60°F (16°C), the aromas, tastes, and sensations of a cider are stronger and any flaws are more noticeable. (See chapter 6 for more on the most common flaws.) Acidity is particularly temperature sensitive. Use the thermometer to ensure the cider is at the proper temperature.

When the cider reaches 60°F (16°C), you are ready to begin tasting.

THE TASTING PROCESS

Rinsing the tasting glass

Begin the tasting process by pouring a small amount of cider into each of the tasting glasses. Swirl the cider around in the glass and then dump the cider into the spit bucket. This removes any foreign aromas. If you are tasting multiple ciders in one sitting, it's important to take this step between each one to avoid blending the ciders.

Now pour about 1.5 ounces (44 ml) of cider into each glass. This is the cider you will be evaluating.

Appearance

First, evaluate the appearance. Although the appearance of a cider does not always correlate with its other characteristics, making a brief note about the color—honey, straw, gold, or another descriptive that makes sense to you—will familiarize you with the range of hues typical in cider and help you recognize when a cider changes color in the maturing process. You can also note the clarity of the cider: Is it hazy or has it "dropped bright"?

Evaluating the cider's appearance

Swirling the cider before smelling it

Nose

Next you will evaluate the aroma, or nose. Swirl the cider in the glass to more fully release the aromas. Empty your mind of any preconceptions and smell the cider.

This is not a quick process. You may smell the cider for a minute or more, identifying different aromas and finding the right words to describe each of them.

In the cider room at Poverty Lane Orchards, the tasters begin calling out the aromas they smell. Because the cidermakers have been tasting together for a long time, they are comfortable agreeing with, refining, clarifying, or disagreeing with a description offered by someone else at the table. This process of verbalizing their notes has helped them develop a precise vocabulary for the tastings, a boon when you are tasting as many batches over as many years as they have.

For novice tasters, however, it may be best to start silently, with each taster writing down his or her notes before discussion begins. This prevents one taster's experience from overwhelming the others'; the power of suggestion is strong.

Once you have smelled the cider, begin making notes. You will quickly notice that the aroma of cider is layered. There are certain scents that you experienced first and others that came later, regardless of the relative strength of those aromas. The goal is to list the aromas in the order you experienced them. If you don't have the exact word for an aroma, list an approximate description with a questions mark as you experience it, and then return to it when you've completed the list. Stick your nose back in the glass and hunt for it again. Can you find a better description for it?

In this part of the process, conversation can be helpful. Describe the aroma in any terms that occur to you: a color, a sound, a sensation, or a memory. Your fellow tasters may recognize what you are describing and be able to help narrow in on a word. You want to be as exact as possible. Do you smell orange? Can you be more specific? Is it a navel orange or a clementine? Is it orange peel or orange juice or orange marmalade or orange popsicle?

As you taste you will develop a vocabulary of words that are unique to you and your fellow tasters. During a Farnum Hill Ciders tasting, the term *BSA* is often used. BSA is shorthand for *bittersweet apples* and describes the distinctive pear-like, leathery aroma of bins of bittersweet apples in storage. It is an aroma that the Poverty Lane Orchards crew is very familiar with, but it is unlikely that you, as a home cidermaker, have the same point of reference. You probably won't use the term *BSA* in your tasting notes; instead, you'll be challenged to find other words, with meaning to you and your fellow tasters, to describe the same experience.

Remember: You have a whole world of aromas to draw from—and not just food-related aromas. The Farnum Hill Ciders tasting notes are filled with comments about sweat and manure. (And those aren't necessarily bad things.)

Evaluating the cider's nose

CIDERMAKING TIP

Resetting Your Sense of Smell

Your nose can get tired. It becomes accustomed to the smell of cider during the course of a tasting and is no longer as sensitive to its aromas. To reset their sense of smell, the Farnum Hill Ciders tasters rely on two tricks:

• Rubbing the bridge of the nose

• Smelling themselves, often by ducking their nose into their shirt

No one knows exactly why these actions reawaken the sense of smell, but they've helped the crew through long tastings. Sometimes though, a taster's perceptions will be off no matter what tricks you use. During a Farnum Hill tasting, that's known as being "broken." Try again tomorrow.

Tasting the cider

Taking notes at a tasting

Taste

Human taste buds are a far more limited tool than you imagine them to be. The tongue can only perceive acid, bitter, sweet, sour, salty, and savory flavors. Your sense of "taste" is truly your nose at work again, perceiving the changing aromas of a food in your mouth. (For evidence, try tasting with your nose plugged.) This scientific distinction, however, is not all that important for cider tasting. In the tasting process, all of the tastes and aromas that you experience when you first put the cider in your mouth are considered to be the cider's taste.

Taste the cider by drawing a small amount into your mouth. Don't swallow it. Swirl it around and spit it into the spit bucket. This is akin to rinsing the glass. Now draw a mouthful into your mouth. Again: Don't swallow the cider. Instead swirl it around to coat your mouth (this time because different parts of the tongue are more sensitive to different flavors) and suck in some air through your lips to aerate it. This takes some practice—and sounds silly—but the air helps release the aromas in your mouth.

Start by evaluating the acidity and bitterness of the cider. These are perceived by the tongue alone. Which of the two hits your senses first? How quickly does the other arrive? Cider tasting notes often read: "Acid over bitter" or "acid and bitter in balance." Then describe the acidity and bitterness.

Because these are not aromas or flavors in the way they are usually defined, it can be difficult to find descriptive words. Most often, the Farnum Hill cidermakers use shape, size, or sensation descriptors. The acid may be "bright," "round," "sharp," or "flat." The bitter may be "broad," "direct," or "moderate," among the many other descriptions that fill years of notebooks.

Now, describe the taste as you experience it. List the flavors in the order they appear, as you did with the aromas. Aim for precision in your description—"white grape," "lemonade," "lime zest," "fruit cocktail," "compost," "leather," "lumber"—without worrying that you've never tasted some of them.

CIDERMAKING TIP

Tasting Process

Follow these steps, taking notes along the way, to evaluate ciders objectively.

1. Pour a small amount of cider into the tasting glass. Swirl and discard.
2. Pour about 1.5 ounces (4 ml) of cider into the tasting glass for evaluation.
3. Evaluate the appearance. Note the color and clarity.
4. Swirl the cider.
5. Evaluate the nose. Note the aromas in the order you experience them.
6. Taste a small amount of cider. Swirl it in your mouth and spit.
7. Taste a mouthful of cider, swirl it around, and aerate it. Don't swallow.
8. Evaluate the taste. Note the acidity and bitterness. Note the flavors in the order you experience them.
9. Evaluate the mouthfeel. Note the fullness and the astringency.
10. Spit the cider.
11. Evaluate the finish. Note the flavors in the order you experience them.

Mouthfeel

Next consider the mouthfeel. Mouthfeel is the sensation of cider in the mouth. Specifically, you are evaluating the body of the cider and its astringency.

Astringency is different from bitterness, which is perceived by the tongue. Astringency is often described as a drying sensation in the mouth and is related to the tannins present. Describing these properties is straightforward once you have some experience tasting, as they are typically described in relative terms. The body of the cider is usually said to be "light," "medium," or "full." The astringency is described on a scale from "slightly" to "moderately" to "very" astringent.

Like the evaluation of the nose, evaluating the taste and mouthfeel can be a several-minute process. If you want to, spit your first mouthful into the spit bucket and taste again to identify that elusive flavor.

Some tasters will swallow a small amount of cider, believing that the flavors change as they are swallowed (as in beer tasting), but most spit as you would in a wine tasting. Spitting is an important part of the tasting process when you are tasting several ciders. The alcohol content of the cider is enough to change your perceptions as you go through the tasting process. Even when you do spit, a long tasting can wear you down.

Finish

After you spit the cider, you will taste its lingering effects, the "finish." Most often, you'll hear tasters say, "the finish follows," meaning that the finish is a continuation of the taste of the cider. Sometimes, however, one taste will dominate the finish. Approach the finish the same way you approached the taste of the cider. Start by evaluating the acidity and bitterness. Which is apparent first? Then describe the flavors in the order you experience them, with attention to the differences between the taste and the finish. Does a flavor that was behind the scenes in the taste dominate in the finish? Does a flavor that was prominent in the taste disappear in the finish?

The word *clean* may be applied to the finish. In cider-tasting speak *clean* means that the cider is free of microbial defects and that the funkier, darker aromas and flavors of the nose have dissipated in the finish, leaving a bright, pleasant aftertaste.

TRAINING
YOUR NOSE

Tasting takes practice. The best way to learn to confidently describe ciders is just to sit down and do it. Over time, you will develop your own vocabulary for the aromas, tastes, and sensations of cider.

You can also work to train your nose and your mind to identify scents more readily. Pay attention to the scents around you and the things that you eat every day and put words to those experiences. Everyone has his or her own methods for storing the information. For instance, some people, while smelling a honeydew melon, will repeat the word *honeydew* in their heads to solidify the mental connection. When you smell something interesting, seek out the source. A bouquet of flowers has a general smell, but each type of flower in the arrangement has a unique one. Smell each flower until you've located the hard-to-identify aroma and make a mental note of the experience.

Tasting Vocabulary

The cidermaker's goal is to develop a consistent and specific vocabulary to objectively describe the aromas, sensations, and tastes in each batch of cider. This way, you can compare batches of cider. In the cider room at Poverty Lane Orchards, a consistent vocabulary allows the cidermakers to discuss the nuances of each batch.

The goal is to be as exacting as possible when choosing words to describe the cider. Try to avoid general terms, such as sweet, floral, earthy, or citrus.

If you smell citrus, stop and ask yourself: What kind of citrus? Once you've focused in on lemon, consider what part of the fruit you are smelling. Is it the peel, the pith, the pulp? Is it a common lemon or a Meyer lemon? Does it smell cooked or sweetened? Would lemon curd or lemonade be a more apt description? Or perhaps you are experiencing a faux lemon aroma. Is it more lemon candy or lemon furniture polish?

Your vocabulary will be unique to you and your fellow tasters—a reflection of your experiences. Following are just some of the terms that have become a part of the vocabulary at Poverty Lane Orchards. As you become a more-experienced taster, you may add descriptive words unique to your cider-tasting experience.

Apricot	Dried leaves	Mango	Rose petals
Balsa wood	Dry twigs	Orange blossom	Scotch
Banana peel	Ferns	Orange juice	Solvent
Bing cherries	Forest floor	Orange peel	Strawberries
Black tea	Furniture	Orangina	Sweet decay
Bread	FYM (farmyard manure)	Overripe orange	Tart cherries
Brine	Green banana	Peach	Tropical jelly
Brown sugar	Green olives	Peach pit	Vanilla
BSA (bittersweet apples)	Green twigs	Pear	Vodka
Burnt matches	Guava	Pear skin	Warm spices
Butterscotch	Hefeweizen beer	Pineapple	Waterfall
Chocolate	Honey	Pomegranate	Whiskey
Compost	Leather	Pond	White grape
Cooked beets	Lime	PWLEO sweat (People Who Like Each Other)	Work sweat
Cream	Lime peel	Quinine	Worry sweat
Dried apricot	Lumber		

DEFINING WHAT YOU LIKE

The tasting process is designed to be an objective one, but the end goal is subjective: The tasting process is a tool to help you create a cider you like. After you have objectively evaluated the ciders, review your notes. Which of the ciders did you like? Which of the ciders didn't you like? What do the ciders in each category have in common?

The more you understand your own likes and dislikes, the easier it will be for you to make decisions about the types of apples you use in your cidermaking (see chapter 3) and your goals if you choose to blend cider (see chapter 7). The knowledge will also help you pick a cider you like from the shelves of your local liquor store while you wait for your own batch of cider to ferment or mature.

OTHER PEOPLE'S CIDER

The crew at Poverty Lane Orchards regularly taste their own cider as well as other people's cider (OPC), to learn from fellow cidermakers' successes and mistakes. The ciders listed here all share the cidermaking philosophy that cider should be an expression of the apple, but differ greatly in their approach to cidermaking and the desired result. If you have access to these ciders through your local liquor store, taste them yourself—remembering that cider varies from year to year—and make notes before reading on. If you don't have access to these particular ciders, practice tasting on others available in your area. Following are Poverty Lane Orchards' notes on tasting the featured ciders.

The distinct processes for making each of these ciders are outlined in chapter 7.

Still Cider—Farnum Hill Dooryard Still Cider 1312 (7.5% ABV)

Label and Website Description

From the label: "Farnum Hill 'Dooryard Still' refers to the big central yard at our home orchard . . . the label presents various nonbubbly dry ciders, some with rowdy tannins, some with edgy notes rare in U.S. ciders."

From the website: "1312 is still, altogether dry, a lucky blend of several 2012 fermentations. Its tannic structure comes chiefly from Dabinett, Yarlington Mill, Major, and Somerset Redstreak; its fruitiness from Golden Russet; its acidity from Wickson, Ashmead's Kernel, and Esopus Spitzenberg. Aroma through finish, we find peach and apricot (fresh and dried), pineapple, various citrus fruits, pear, smoke, and rocks, with pleasingly dynamic acid, tannin and fruit throughout."

Tasting Notes

Appearance: Mid-straw, dead still, clear.

Nose: Peach, apricot (fresh and dried), orange and peel, marmalade, pear, smoke, rocks, grapefruit and peel, citron, dried leaves, leather (bittersweet apple), distant farmyard manure, lemon/lemon oil, general citrus, mango, papaya, faint stinky cheese, maybe horse, lime and peel, dust, wood (not oak), roses (the day before discard?), pineapple.

Taste: Bright acid in balance with broad bitter. Faint implied sweetness. Fresh and dried fruits from nose, especially citrus, citrus peels, dried apricot, peach, prominent bittersweet apple and pear, wood (not oak), broad distant funk in background (cheese/barnyard/dried leaves), behind acid/bitter and fruit.

Feel: Moderately full, moderately astringent.

Finish: Acid and bitter carry in balance, with fruits and funk from nose and taste. A bit more dried fruit, especially apricot, at the end. Clean.

French-style *Cidre*—E.Z. Orchards Willamette Valley *Cidre* 2011 (6% ABV)

Label Description
"E.Z. Orchards *cidre* consists of a blend of vintage French *cidre* apple varieties that we grow in our Willamette Valley orchards. Our fermentation method, like the traditional French *méthode champenoise*, enhances mature apple aroma, is low in acidity and finished with a soft effervescence. Chill upright before serving. To enhance clarity, pour gently to reserve the lees sediment at the bottom of the bottle."

Tasting Notes
Appearance: Copper. Faint haze. Tiny rising bubbles.

Nose: Dried apricot and papaya, dried cranberry and cherry, peach, faintly acetic (nice vinegar), dried fruit/homemade fruit leather, cotton candy, avocado, wood, farmyard manure, orange and peels, brown sugar, lemon juice, horses, lanolin, peach pit, stewed pineapple, lime and seltzer, cream/orange and cream, acid heat, bark, forest floor, dried leaves.

Taste: Acid over sweet over bitter. Slightly acetic in mouth. Lime and seltzer, all fruits from nose (particularly dried cherry and cranberry), with vitamins, fish oil (taste, not smell), fresh and cooked apples.

Mouthfeel: Quite full, moderately astringent.

Finish: Acid and bitter in balance. Fruits from taste carry mostly in balance, animals fade. Strong peach. Clean.

Méthode Champenoise Cider—Eve's Cidery Bittersweet (9% ABV)

Label Description
"This cider is made from a blend of traditional English, French and American cider apples. Like wine grapes, true cider apples have an ideal balance of tannins, acid and sugar needed to produce a fermented beverage. A secondary bottle fermentation creates natural carbonation. Golden, bubbly and semi-dry, Bittersweet is crisp and fruity with a hint of earthy tannins. Pairs well with most food. Served chilled."

Tasting Notes
Appearance: Pale gold, rising bubbles, clear.

Nose: Apple concentrate, apples in cold storage. Sweet and tart. Pear. Fructose, grapefruit, McIntosh and baked apple, sweet fruit cocktail, vanilla, nutmeg and warm spice, cooked tropical fruits, guava paste/jam. Very concentrated fruit. Fried bananas, coconut (shell), cooked winter squash, green leaves, strawberry, warm pineapple.

Taste: Sweet, but more tart than expected from nose. Strong acid, sweet, then bitter. Mom's apple pie, fresh bread/bakery (yeast), boiled apple cider, citrus peels, pink grapefruit, strawberry and leaves.

Mouthfeel: Full, moderate-high astringency, very fizzy.

Finish: Faithfully follows nose and taste. Acid and sweetness carry, bitter balanced in background. Apple (fresh, cooked, stored, and boiled), pear, guava jam, warm spice, warming alcohol. Clean.

Ice Cider—Eden Vermont Ice Cider Heirloom Blend (10% ABV)

Label Description
"Made from a unique blend of traditional and heirloom apple varieties, this delicious ice cider has a complex, balanced flavor and a long finish. 100% of the apples used are grown in Vermont. In addition to McIntosh and Empires, Russets proved full-bodied sweetness, Caville Blanc provides acidity and citrus notes for balance and Ashmead's Kernel provides natural tannins for structure. Serve it with artisanal cheeses, charcuteries and desserts with autumn spices."

Tasting Notes

Appearance: Gold. Dead still. Clear.

Nose: Apple, pear, lemon oil, alcohol, very ripe peach, dried apricot, boiled cider, wood/furniture, green twigs/ sappy springtime note, cream, beeswax, wet dead leaves, sweet cherry, pipe tobacco, orange oil, candied orange peel, candied citrus, whiskey sour, oak barrel/vanilla, candied ginger, mulled tart fruits.

Taste: Acid, sweet, tiny bitter follows. Acid in good balance with sugar. Apples in all stages, pop of quinine and strong tea, rich dried fruits (apricot, mango), boiled cider, very faint cedar. General fruit for miles.

Mouthfeel: Very full, rich, barely astringent, nice acid sting.

Finish: Acid and sweetness carry in balance with all fruits from taste, strong black tea underneath. Clean.

After the harvest

Tasting Cider

Anyone who makes food or drink should learn how to evaluate their product. Tasting is really nothing more than an effort to objectify characteristics that are essentially subjective, at least well enough to enable those of us who grow the apples and make ciders to speak intelligently to one another. It's no use to gather the crew together over a glass of cider to mutter, "This is pretty good. We should try to make it better." All the tedious, pretentious wine (and food) language that wrecks so many dinner conversations is based on something real: an effort by professionals to speak to one another in a language that has objective meaning.

When we first started making cider, we had no clue about tasting. I started to spend a fair bit of time at winemakers' sensory analysis sessions. We took a cider industry tasting class in the UK. None of this really taught us exactly how to taste, but we began to understand that regular people could learn how to do this, and we were encouraged to start tasting cider in a more rigorous way. In the late 1990s, five of us began to meet for regular tasting sessions, in the late morning, around our dining room table. We blinded ourselves to what we tasted, and we wrote our own individual notes in silence before we spoke. We structured our work very tightly and examined five elements in every sample: appearance, nose, taste, mouthfeel, and finish.

After a couple of years of this effort, we gained the confidence that we could taste together and speak as we worked, with only one person writing. That's what we do today. We still follow the same structured approach and have developed an evolving descriptive language that is very useful to us at every stage of our job. We have the good fortune of a collective sensory memory; three of the five who started doing this together are still here. Others come and go. But we almost always have a handful of people around who have learned the rudiments of tasting. Among other things, we've learned that almost anyone with a healthy nose, tongue, imagination, and command of language can do this quite well.

We taste at every step of cidermaking, from the orchard to the bottle. We bite and spit apples in the orchards as they ripen. We taste them again at the press, as they're being blended and turned into juice. We taste the juice on its way to fermentation. But the really hard tasting job begins once the ciders have finished fermentation when we need to begin blending finished ciders.

We have reams of tasting notes from years of work. But you won't see these notes on the backs of our bottles. Once it's in the bottle, we don't want to ruin the party by encouraging someone to drone on about dried apricot, guava, leather, and soft cheese elements in our cider. We want it to be sipped, enjoyed, and used to lubricate conversations on more interesting topics.

3

Starting with Apples

Cider begins in the orchard. Very few home cidermakers pick and press their own apples, and even fewer grow their own apples, so you might be tempted to skip this chapter. Don't. Home cidermakers who will buy the juice for cidermaking from an orchard still need to understand the apple. Apples are the main—and some would say the only—ingredient in cider.

Buy the highest quality juice you can find for your home cidermaking. That's the best advice you can get about cidermaking. The difference high-quality ingredients will have on the finished product is dramatic. Don't buy apple juice in the supermarket to make cider. Overlooking issues of quality, store-bought juice often has additives that make fermentation difficult or impossible.

IN THE ORCHARD

Every decision an apple grower makes—from what varieties of apple trees to plant to how close to plant those trees to one another—affects the fruit that the trees produce and the cider that you can make from them.

For that reason, smaller orchards focused on growing cider apples look very different from commercial orchards growing dessert apples, as apples designed for eating are called. Commercial orchards growing dessert apples often plant small trees very densely, with as many as 1,000 trees per acre (0.4 ha). The trees, often irrigated, are flanked by grassless strips of dirt that allow more water and nutrients to flow to the trees and prevent pests, and the apples are picked from the tree before they achieve complete ripeness, with the prettiest apples fetching the highest prices.

It is often said that the bin of apples that looks the worst is worth the most. Cider apples are not judged on the same criteria as dessert apples. Apples don't have to be attractive or consistently sized to have a great flavor.

In the bittersweet cider apple orchards at Poverty Lane, apples are grown on big trees, planted just 200 trees to the acre (0.4 ha), and grass flanks the trees. The orchard looks like the classic New England farm that it is, but these decisions serve an apple-growing purpose. For instance, the grass provides a soft landing for the cider apples, most of which are picked off the ground.

When growing cider apples you are looking for extremely ripe fruit, just on the edge of rot. The texture of the apple may be soft or chewy, but that isn't a concern in a process that involves pressing the apples for the juice. For the cidermaker, the key is picking apples after all the fruits' starch has been converted to sugars.

Planting apple trees

Spring in the Orchard

Making a batch of cider is, in truth, a yearlong process. The process begins in late winter or early spring as the apple trees, which have been dormant for the winter, begin to awaken. As the weather begins to warm, the tight, scaly buds of the winter apple tree begin to swell in anticipation of spring.

At the orchard, the winter and early spring are a time to prune the trees, grooming them for a fruitful growing season. As the days grow warmer and the ground thaws, the pruning brush is turned into mulch to nourish the soil and the trees. New apple trees are also planted in the first days of spring; it will be several years before those new trees produce an apple crop. Some varieties will produce a good crop in the third "leaf," or year; others won't produce a full crop until the eighth leaf.

Spring is a time of rapid change in the apple orchard. First, the long-dormant trees develop a light gray fur on their scaly buds. This is known as "silver tip." Next, the trees show "green tip," a tiny sliver of green on the buds. A few days later, you will see "quarter-inch (6 mm) green" and then "half-inch (1.3 cm) green," as the buds continue to grow. If you look closely you will see that each flash of green is a cluster of four or five buds gathered tightly around a central bud. If you were to dissect one of the buds, you would see flower organs developing.

For the apple growers—particularly ones who practice a minimal-intervention approach to pest management—observing the orchard carefully is key. It's important to understand how the weather and other environmental factors are affecting the trees, and to watch out for signs of pests or other enemies of the orchard that might affect the season's burgeoning crop.

Next, the trees begin to produce leaves. "Mouse ear" is the term for the moment the first tiny green leaves pop out. They do resemble mouse ears. Next, the "tight cluster" of buds separates slightly. This is called "floret separation."

The progression of an apple tree's growth through a gently warming spring is predictable, but no less dramatic for that. Shortly after "floret separation" comes "king pink," when the center bud cracks, revealing a hint of pink. Depending on the weather, every bud will turn pink within a day or two, a stage known as "full pink." The surest sign that spring has arrived comes shortly thereafter, when the center bud blooms, "king blossom." Within a week, the apple orchard will be awash in blooms, a beautiful moment known as "full bloom."

This is a critical moment for the apple trees, which must be pollinated to produce apples. Bees and other insects attracted by the nectar of the apple blossoms spread the pollen from tree to tree; most apple trees are not self-pollinating, which means they must receive pollen from another apple tree, not simply from another flower on the same tree. Apple growers hope for sunny, fair weather during full bloom. Rain and wind can damage the blossoms and discourage the bees and other insects.

After this period of pollination, the trees lose their bloom—"petal fall"—and tiny apples, just an eighth of an inch (3 mm), begin to form. If you dissect these tiny fruits, you can see their developing seeds, a sign that pollination occurred. If pollination has not occurred, the tiny fruit will simply fall from the tree.

Summer in the Orchard

As the trees begin to produce apples, some will fall from the tree. This is the tree deciding how many apples it can support for the season. The apple grower often intervenes in this process. Frequently, an apple grower will further thin the crop to ensure the tree can produce high-quality, and not just high-quantity, fruit. The apple grower also has ways to encourage a larger crop from trees that are under producing. A tree that is strategically damaged will often be shocked into producing more apples.

Through the summer, the orchardist is on careful watch to prevent or eradicate pests, from apple scab to deer. Many apple growers will run leaf and soil tests to evaluate when the trees should be fertilized. And there is always mowing and pruning to be done.

Warm and sunny summer days with the occasional soaking evening rain are the apple growers' ideal through the summer months. Passing afternoon thundershowers are their nightmare. Extreme conditions during a thunderstorm, especially hail, can damage trees, but the bright sunlight that comes after the storm, intensified through the magnifying-glasslike lens of each raindrop, is also a danger, threatening heat damage.

Summer at the orchard

Fall in the Orchard

As the summer days shorten into fall, the apple grower hopes for drier weather and a slow and steady temperature decline. The wish for drier weather is for the apple growers' well-being as well as for the trees': Harvest comes with many outdoor chores.

The size of the harvest depends on innumerable variables, but the weather is key. No season is ideal, but the hardest seasons for the apple grower and the apple trees are ones with extreme temperature changes or weather events. Nothing confuses a tree more than a stretch of warm days in the middle of winter or a cold snap in July.

Cider apples are most often picked from the ground. The apples fall from the tree at the peak of ripeness and those that don't release their hold as easily are loosened with a gentle tap to the tree with a long pole. A tree is picked several times over the course of a week to ten days; each time the pickers, working by hand, take only the ripest fruit.

In American cider orchards, most apples are picked by hand. In European cider orchards, harvest is more often mechanical. One machine shakes the trunk of the tree, sending the apples to the ground, and another collects the apples.

Different apple varieties mature at different rates, so picking can occur from the early fall through the late fall. Because Poverty Lane Orchards is located in the cold climates of northern New England, this can mean that the late-harvest apples are exposed to temperatures well below freezing during the nights. Cidermakers who work with this type of fruit believe that these frosts—but not a deep freeze—improve the fruit.

Harvesting cider apples

Winter at the orchard

Winter in the Orchard

When the deep freeze comes, the work in the orchard comes to a halt. The trees prepare for hibernation, throwing off their leaves and developing a scaly covering to protect the buds. There is plenty of winter pruning to be done, but in the cider orchard the attention turns from the apple trees to the cider room.

THE APPLE

The apple tree produces apples for the purposes of spreading the apple seeds hidden inside the fruit. In a natural environment, the sweet fruit attracts animals that eat and excrete the seeds. The cidermaker interrupts this process, taking the apples for the purpose of cidermaking, not seed distribution.

Most home cidermakers start the cidermaking process with juice, but a basic understanding of the terms used to describe apples can be helpful. When talking about apples, apple growers most often consider the size—apples can range in size from tiny ¾-inch (2 cm) fruit to 3¾-inch (9 cm) fruit—shape, skin, and flesh of the apple.

An apple's shape is often described as conical (tall and tapered from the shoulders, or stem end, to the calyx, or bloom end), cylindrical (tall and untapered) or flat (more broad than tall). Shape is typically a lesser concern for cidermakers.

The skin of an apple contains some of the flavor, aromas, and other compounds that will make their way into the juice and the cider. The skin can be described by feel (smooth or rough, dry or oily), thickness (thick or thin) and, most often, color. Apples start their growing life as green fruit and then develop a variety of colors from green to yellow, orange, and red. Apples are often described has having a background or "ground" color and a surface or blush color. This combination of colors can give apples a striped, splotched, or streaked appearance. Some varieties of apples are also described as being "russeted," which means they have a brownish, leathery layer on the skin. The color of the skin does not affect the juice and cider, but the tannins and other compounds present in the skin can shape the cider.

The flesh of a ripe apple contains most of the flavors, aromas, and other compounds, such as tannins and acids, that will be found in the pressed juiced and the fermented cider. The texture of the flesh can be described as fine grained (sometimes considered "greasy" in pressing) or grainy (which can be "dry" in pressing). Its flavors, and the acids and tannins, can be described in numerous ways. (See chapter 2.)

A SAMPLING OF APPLES

Because apples are an agricultural product, where and how the apples are grown can have a big impact on their taste and texture. You won't find all of these apples—or these exact apple characteristics—in your region, but this sampling will give you a taste of the apples grown by Farnum Hill and other leading cidermakers around the world and how they are used in cidermaking.

Typically, cidermakers mix the juice of several apple varieties harvested around the same time before beginning fermentation. Only a few varieties have all the necessary characteristics to produce a balanced cider on their own.

When cidermakers talk about apples, they often divide them into two loose, unofficial categories: cider apples and commercial apples. The first category is for those apples that are grown primarily for cidermaking. The home cidermaker usually has to seek these apples out from small, local producers, but the effort is rewarded with more nuanced, balanced cider. Commercial apples are more easily accessible to the home cidermaker; commercial apples are often divided into dessert or eating apples and baking apples. Although many common apples are not suited for cidermaking, varieties such as Golden Delicious, Idared, and Jonathan are widely available. These apples have properties which make them a reasonable stand-in for more traditional cider

Idared

apples. Taste the apples to evaluate their usefulness in cidermaking.

Cidermakers divide "cider apples" further into categories that describe their main characteristics: bitter-sweet, which provide tannins; bittersharps, which provide both acid and tannins; sweets, which provide flavor and aroma; and sharps, which provide acid.

If the exact varieties listed below aren't widely grown in your region or did not produce a large crop this season, don't despair. If you think about balance and select apples that will provide the necessary sugars, acid, tannins, and flavors you can create a good cider from the available fruit.

As a note: Both early- and late-season apples can produce delicious, balanced cider. However, early-season apples tend to produce ciders with lower alcohol content than late-season apples.

Ashton Bitter

Dabinett

Ellis Bitter

Bittersweet Cider Apples

Bittersweet apples provide a cider's structure. Their tannins can make them unpleasant for eating out of hand, but those same tannins provide the underpinnings for a good batch of cider. Tannins are responsible for the astringent and bitter characteristics in cider. Generally, cidermakers are looking for two types of tannins: soft tannins, such as those found in Yarlington Mill, and harsher tannins, such as those found in Dabinett. Bittersweet apples are low in acid, so they are blended with other, more acidic apples to create a balanced cider.

Ashton Bitter

A popular early-season apple in England in the 1970s and '80s, Ashton Bitter has a squashed, conical shape with orangey-red stripes on a yellow background. The Ashton Bitter apple tree does not produce the sizeable crops needed for large-scale commercial cidermaking, but has value for small-batch cidermaking.

Apple flesh: A balance between fine-grained and grainy, under a thick skin

Apple flavor: Very harsh tannins, with only a faint apple taste

Use in cidermaking: Harsher tannins in early-season cidermaking

Chisel Jersey

Like Dabinett, Chisel Jersey is an old English variety. Some believe the two apples to be related. Chisel Jersey has a similar shape and coloring and ripens at the same time, but its tannins are even more aggressive than the harsh Dabinett tannins.

Apple flesh: Somewhat grainy

Apple flavor: Direct, astringent tannins with leather and citrusy fruit flavors in the background

Use in cidermaking: Harsher tannins. (Surprisingly, though, the juice of the Chisel Jersey is less tannic than the apple, and after fermentation more fruity flavors emerge.)

Dabinett

This old English bittersweet originated in Somerset County in the early 1900s. Today, the cold-hardy apple remains a mainstay of traditional English ciders. The slightly flattened orange- and red-striped apple is hard to eat, but its notably harsh tannins are exactly what make it a popular cider apple.

Apple flesh: Somewhat grainy; can be dry when pressed

Apple flavor: The first thing that strikes you is hard tannins, bitter and astringent, followed by leather and apple flavors.

Use in cidermaking: Prized for its tannins; a workhorse apple for Farnum Hills' late-season ciders

Ellis Bitter

Held in high regard by cidermakers as a versatile apple, Ellis Bitter traces its origin to nineteenth-century England. To the untrained eye, the conical, orange-red apples resemble Major apples.

Apple flesh: A balance between fine-grained and grainy

Apple flavor: Middle-of-the-road tannins

Use in cidermaking: A good all-purpose apple that keeps well, often used to balance early fermentations

Harry Masters Jersey

A conical, pale red, English apple, sometimes called Port Wine, Harry Masters Jersey resembles Yarlington Mill in flavor and use. It matures earlier in the season than Yarlington Mill.

Apple flesh: Fine-grained; the apples mill easily, but can be loose or "greasy" in pressing

Apple flavor: Similar to Yarlington Mill with soft tannins

Use in cidermaking: Softer tannins in early- to mid-season cidermaking

Major

Commonly found in old farm orchards of Devon and south Somerset, these English apples have soft tannins often used to balance the hasher tannins of many bittersweets.

Apple flesh: A balance between fine-grained and grainy; presses easily

Apple flavor: Soft, round tannins and fruity characteristics

Use in cidermaking: Softer tannins in early-season cidermaking

Medaille d'Or

A late blooming but early ripening French apple, Medaille d'Or has a tough golden yellow skin covered in

Medaille d'Or

brown russet. The apple is tiny, but the tannins are huge.

Apple flesh: Grainy

Apple flavor: So bitter and astringent as to make other bittersweet apples seem mild in comparison

Use in cidermaking: Extremely harsh tannins in early-season cidermaking; used sparingly

Somerset Redstreak

For apple growers, Somerset Redstreak is a frustrating biennial variety. A plentiful crop one season promises a scarce one the next. The beautiful, small, red apple should not be confused with the older, similarly named Redstreak, a bittersharp variety.

Apple flesh: A balance between fine-grained and grainy

Apple flavor: Although the tannins can vary based on growing conditions, they are usually softer.

Use in cidermaking: Beautiful, softer tannins in early-season cidermaking

Yarlington Mill

Yarlington Mill

Another classic English cider apple, Yarlington Mill has been a popular blending apple for more than a hundred years. The reddish-pink apple is tall, tapering toward the calyx. Yarlington Mill apples have softer tannins than many bittersweets, which means the apples have a less aggressively bitter bite when tasted.

Apple flesh: Fine-grained; the apples mill easily, but can be loose or "greasy" in pressing

Apple flavor: Soft, round tannin with subtle fruit flavors and less leathery flavor than many bittersweets

Use in cidermaking: Softer tannins in mid- and late-season cidermaking; Farnum Hill often blends Yarlington Mill with the more harshly tannic Dabinett.

Bittersharp Cider Apples

Bittersharp apples are high in both acid and tannins, though the tannins are typically not as aggressive as those found in bittersweet apples.

Foxwhelp

The name Foxwhelp dates to the 1600s, but it's unlikely that cider-makers today are fermenting the same Foxwhelp apples as their English forerunners. In the intervening centuries, the name has been applied to numerous varieties of apples, including H. P. Bulmer's Improved Foxwhelp.

Apple flesh: The most common modern variety is a large apple with soft flesh.

Apple flavor: The green apple with red stripes has less astringency and bitterness than many bittersharps.

Use in cidermaking: The mid-season apple can be useful in blending.

Kingston Black

Kingston Black is notable for being one of the few cider apples grown today that will make a delicious cider all on its own. The small, deep red apple, which originated in England's Somerset County in the nineteenth century, has a balance of sugar, tannins, and tartness.

Apple flesh: Moderately grainy; easy to press

Foxwhelp

Kingston Black

Apple flavor: Considered by some to be an edible apple, with structured, but not harsh tannins and a light sourness

Use in cidermaking: Often fermented by itself, producing a barely acidic cider with reasonable tannic underpinnings

Redstreak

Like Foxwhelp, the English Redstreak apple is a subject of much lore and confusion. Centuries-old cider texts describe an ideal cider apple, with all the attributes necessary for creating a well-balanced, single-variety cider. For years, cidermakers have searched for that apple. Today's Redstreak has red streaks on a yellowish-green background, but it is a small, unexceptional bittersharp used in blending.

Apple flesh: Mushy when ripe

Apple flavor: Nice, round acidity with some tannic structure

Use in cidermaking: For early season blending. Redstreak can add acid without adding significant flavor.

Stoke Red

Apple growers don't love Stoke Red—the trees are notoriously tricky to grow—but cidermakers are fond of the small, flat, orange-and-red striped apples, which originated in Somerset County, England. Stoke Red are no longer planted widely but, unlike many bittersharps, the current variety is believed to be unchanged from the one cidermakers used a century ago.

Apple flesh: Somewhat grainy; mushy

Apple flavor: Very strong with dominant acidity and harsh tannins

Use in cidermaking: A wonderful source of acid in mid-season blends; produces a low- to medium-alcohol cider.

Sharp Cider Apples

When fermented, sharp cider apples create cider with bright acids and flavors from herbs to fruit to flowers.

Ashmead's Kernel

An old English cider apple that thrives in North America, Ashmead's Kernel is also delicious for eating, with an abundance of fruity and floral flavors. The apple is classically beautiful, round with a flowery calyx and a textured brown russet over an orange-yellow background.

Apple flesh: Very grainy

Apple flavor: The apple's fruity and floral flavors and acid–sugar balance produce a high-alcohol, high-acid cider with rose-like aromas.

Use in cidermaking: Fermented on its own for blending. The finished cider provides floral, fruity acid to late-season blends.

Esopus Spitzenburg

Esopus Spitzenburg originated in Ulster County, New York, in the eighteenth century. The slightly conical, orange-red apple was reputedly a favorite of Thomas Jefferson, who tried, but failed, to cultivate the apple at his home in Virginia. Unlike many cider apples, "Spitz," as it has been nicknamed by fond cidermakers, is also good for eating, cooking, and drying.

Apple flesh: Dense; not grainy

Apple flavor: Intense acid balances out high sugar for a rich apple that

Esopus Spitzenburg

Golden Russet

produces green herblike flavors in fermentation.

Use in cidermaking: Spitz produces a high-alcohol cider that is also high in soft, bright acids, making it a favorite for late-season blends.

Wickson

This tart, red apple was developed on the West Coast for cidermaking. Its small size means that it is rarely grown for eating, but it is a tasty treat fresh as well as in cider.

Apple flesh: Fine-grained; crisp, white, and juicy

Apple flavor: This herbal, spicy apple creates a pale, aromatic, high-acid cider that suggests white grapes.

Use in cidermaking: Fermented on its own for blending. The finished cider provides grapelike acid to mid- and late-season blends.

Sweet Cider Apples

Sweet cider apples are often less coveted than their high acid or high tannin counterparts, but they can add sweet, fruity flavors to cider.

Golden Russet

Golden Russet apples are round with a flowery calyx and a sweet, fruity flavor with acid. For the home cider-maker, Golden Russet may be one of the easiest-to-find fruits that can be fermented alone into a fruity, low-acid cider that develops complexity through maturation.

Apple flesh: Yellow; slightly chewy

Apple flavor: This generically "fruity" apple can produce cider with flavors of peaches, pears, mangoes, and pineapple.

Use in cidermaking: In blending, Golden Russet adds fruit flavors without changing acidity. Can be fermented alone.

TURNING APPLES INTO JUICE

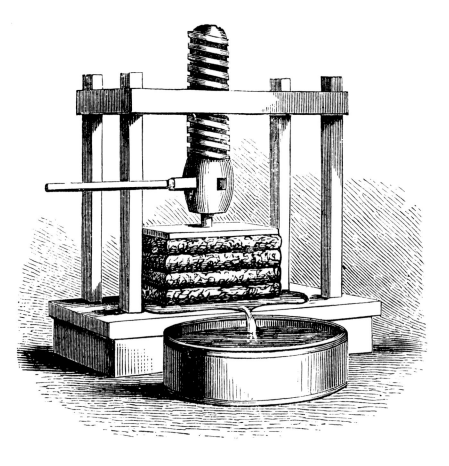

The process of turning apples into juice is a relatively straightforward one: Apples are milled into pomace and then the pomace is pressed to extract the juice. The juice is collected and the pomace is discarded. This process is the same for sweet cider—which can be consumed right off the press—or hard cider, which is then fermented.

There are many different types of mills; some grind the apples while others slice or grate. There are also many different types of presses. At Poverty Lane Orchards, the pomace is pressed in a vertical rack-and-cloth press. The pomace is placed on burlaplike cloth between wooden frames. Slowly, a hydraulic piston rises pressing the pomace. The juice flows out of the pomace, strained by the cloth, and the solids remain behind.

Through the harvest, the orchard's press can produce 800 gallons (3,028 L) of sweet cider a day. Large commercial presses produce tens of thousands of gallons a day. Regardless of the press used, each bushel of apples (a bushel is about 42 pounds, or 19 kg) produces about three gallons (11 L) of juice. The six gallons (23 L) of juice you will use to make your first batch of hard cider started as two bushels, or 84 pounds (38 kg), of apples.

SOURCES
FOR JUICE

For the home cidermaker, finding a source of high-quality juice can be the most difficult part of the cidermaking process. At a minimum, you must start with juice without any additives. Many cidermakers also prefer to use unpasteurized juice (and it is essential for making cider through spontaneous fermentation; see chapter 7) but the sale of unpasteurized cider is regulated.

The key to finding the best juice is asking the right questions. Start by contacting local orchards or home brewing suppliers, which may sell juice from cider apple orchards. Fellow home cidermakers are a good resource for juice sources in your region.

Tell the orchard or home brewing supplier what you are looking for. Because an apple's availability and characteristics can vary by region or growing season, it's easier to talk about the qualities you are looking for—a high level of tannins, for instance—than to ask for specific varieties. It can be easy to get caught up in the lore surrounding different types of apples; don't automatically assume the apples labeled "heirloom" are the best cidermaking apples available. They may not have been bred or cultivated for cidermaking.

If possible try the juice—or the apples—before purchasing six gallons (23 L) for your carboy. You aren't necessarily looking for delicious juice, so don't be seduced by the aromatics that are likely to change during fermentation. Instead, evaluate the balance of sweetness and acidity, and look for noticeable tannins.

Most importantly, though, don't let the quest for the perfect juice prevent you from getting your start as a home cidermaker. Cidermaking is process. Start fermenting with the best juice you can find and continue your hunt for even better juice for the next batch.

An Apple Grower and His Apple Trees

The orchards on Poverty Lane were first planted in the early 1960s, on former crop and grazing land. I started working here in 1965, when I was 11. I was pretty much raised with those trees. I began managing the orchards in 1973, and bought the farm in 1984. One of my earliest jobs was mulching each of 5,000 trees with hay, with a pitchfork. Louisa, long before we were married, spent hard hours on her hands and knees bridge-grafting many of these trees to save them from rodent damage. Our sons, Harry and Otis, grew up sword fighting with applewood sticks in these orchards, and riding on the shoulders of apple pickers. Only a hard person could avoid developing affection for trees he's known for so long.

But it's important to avoid anthropomorphizing old tree friends too much. An apple grower needs to be able to pull trees out of the ground from time to time, to make room for new ones. And an apple grower needs to be willing to make apple trees do his bidding. Apple trees (like Labradors) are among the most forgiving creatures on the earth—they will accommodate all manner of well-intentioned errors by a person with a pruning saw. But it's a mistake to think that they need us. The only reason for a human to do anything to an apple tree is to make it perform a job. We work on the trees for our own sakes, not for theirs.

At Poverty Lane Orchards and Farnum Hill Ciders, we've been working for years to learn how to grow good apples and make delicious cider. The main thing we've learned is that all the best ciders are made in the orchard, not in the cider room. They are made by cidermakers who respect the fruit, the trees, and the land. Many winemakers and cidermakers put their signature on their bottles. We know that if anyone should sign our bottles, it's the trees.

4

Your Cider Room

For the home cidermaker, the equipment and ingredients you need to stock your cider room to produce that first—or fiftieth—batch of cider are simple, inexpensive, easy-to-find, and don't take up much room at all.

At Poverty Lane Orchards, the cider room is an enormous barn with a concrete floor. It is home to a cider press, 275-gallon (1,041 L) plastic tanks of fresh apple juice, towering stainless-steel tanks, and old oak barrels. A table in the middle of the room is piled high with cider bottles, both full and empty, and notebooks filled with handwritten tasting notes. In a closet just big enough for two, is a chemistry lab's worth of glass beakers and tools to measure the characteristics too subtle or important to be left to taste alone. A forklift might rumble by.

Don't worry: Your cider room doesn't need a forklift.

WHERE TO MAKE CIDER

You can make cider almost anywhere—but your decisions about where to make your first batch of cider can affect the final product.

Small-scale cidermaking doesn't require a lot of space. A five- or six-gallon jug (19 or 23 L) typically takes up less than one square foot (929 cm²) of space (you will be using two) and the other cidermaking equipment you will need for your first batch is minimal. Serious cidermakers dedicate a "cider room"—perhaps just a portion of the garage—to their batches. Storing all your cidermaking supplies together like that is convenient, but not necessary.

The most important thing to consider when choosing a place to make cider is temperature.

Temperature

The yeast you will use to ferment your juice and produce cider is temperature sensitive. When the yeast is first introduced into the juice—a process called "pitching"—and for the first several days of the fermentation process, the batch is best stored some place with a consistent temperature of 65°F to 70°F (18°C to 21°C). The yeast will multiply quickly and grow strong at this temperature.

After a few days, when the mixture is bubbling steadily, you will move the batch to the coolest spot you can find for the rest of the fermentation. The cooler temperatures slow the fermentation process, which preserves more of the fruity aromas and flavors of the juice. The fermentation will continue, slowly, at temperatures as low as 35°F (2°C), but most yeast prefers a home that is 40°F to 60°F (4°C to 16°C).

Sometimes this is as simple as starting the batch near your furnace and then moving it to a distant corner of the basement.

Once you have moved the batch to a cool location, it's best to leave it undisturbed until the final steps of the cidermaking process. If, however, the temperature of this cider room suddenly changes—if for instance, your cider room is the rarely heated spare bedroom but you suddenly have houseguests—relocating to another cool space is preferable to overheating the batch.

If you can't find any cool place to store the batch as it ferments, it might be time to reconsider your home cidermaking plans: Would you have more options at a different time of year? Do you want to share the project with a friend who has a better spot for a cider room?

EQUIPMENT

Whether experienced or novice, the cidermaker doesn't need a lot of expensive equipment to make great cider. Buy the following basics from a local or online winemaking or home brewing supplier.

Containers

For your first batch of cider, you will need two containers. The first container is for fermentation. The second (slightly smaller) container is for storing the cider for aging or drinking.

The best choice for the home cidermaker is a glass carboy. A carboy is simply a jug with rigid sides and a narrow neck and mouth. They are available from any home brewing supplier in a variety of sizes, in either plastic or glass. Both materials are suitable for home cidermaking, but a glass carboy is often preferable because it is easier to clean. All carboys are transparent, and will allow the cidermaker to observe the fermentation process better than an opaque vessel.

Some home cidermakers choose to ferment cider in a bucket, also available from a home brewing supplier. Great cider can be made in a bucket, but the process is more prone to error.

The shape of the carboy is its advantage. You'll fill the first carboy almost completely with juice. Because the neck of the carboy is narrow, only a limited amount of juice is exposed to air. In the wide bucket, a much larger amount of juice is exposed. During the fermentation process, the carbon dioxide produced by the yeast forms a protective layer over the developing cider, preventing the cider from coming in contact with oxygen, but when fermentation is complete, the carbon dioxide dissipates, leaving the exposed cider vulnerable to oxidation. The cider in the bucket, with its large surface area, is more at risk.

This same principal explains why you want a smaller, second carboy for storing the cider. When you transfer the cider from the first carboy to the second, you will leave behind the lees—the remnants of the yeast and fruit solids. That means that the volume of cider produced will be less than the volume of the original juice; plus, you will want to taste and evaluate your cider at this point in the process. Because you always want to fill the carboy to the neck when storing finished cider, the second carboy must be smaller than the first.

Glass versus Plastic
Most home cidermaking equipment is available in both plastic and glass versions. It's the cidermaker's choice. Plastic equipment can be more durable, but glass has the advantage of being easier to clean and often higher quality.

When choosing between plastic and glass, consider the tool's use. Plastic is perfect for easily broken tools such as a graduated cylinder, while a glass container is often preferable for fermentation. A glass container allows you to observe the batch throughout the process.

It's important to note that there are many different types of plastic. Some, such as the low-density plastic you find sweet cider packaged in, are not good for storing cider. Others, such as the high-density plastic used to make food-grade buckets, are suitable.

CIDERMAKING TIP

First-Batch Shopping List

- One 6-gallon (23 L) glass carboy
- One 5-gallon (19 L) glass carboy
- Two carboy bungs, one solid and one bored
- Airlock
- Plastic tubing
- Thermometer

- Narrow-range litmus paper
- Hydrometer, measuring specific gravity
- 100-milliliter graduated cylinder
- Plastic crate
- Empty plastic jug
- Bottles and seals, for bottling

- 6 gallons (23 L) of the best apple juice you can find
- Campden tablets
- Red Star Pasteur Champagne yeast or Lalvin DV10 yeast
- Yeast nutrients, optional
- Carboy brush

All the equipment you will need to make cider: 6-gallon (23 L) and 5-gallon (19 L) glass carboys (A), Carboy brush (B), Empty plastic container (C), Carboy bungs (D), Airlock (E), Plastic tubing (F), Hydrometer (G), Thermometer (H), Litmus paper (I), Campden tablets (J), Graduated cylinder (K), Bottles and seals (L), Yeast (M), High-quality apple juice (N), Plastic crate (O)

Carboy Bung

A bung seals the juice in the carboy. You will need two bungs, one solid one and one bored with a hole through the middle for the addition of an airlock. A bung can be made of rubber, silicon, or cork. The only real requirement is a tight fit in the mouth of the carboy.

Airlock

An airlock is used during the fermentation process to let carbon dioxide produced by the yeast escape from the carboy while preventing air from entering. There are two main types of airlocks: an s-shaped airlock and a three-piece airlock. Both function similarly, with water added to the airlock, allowing the carbon dioxide to bubble out, but sealing the carboy against oxidation.

Plastic Tubing

Basic flexible food-grade tubing, available from any wine or home brewing supplier or your local hardware store, is needed to transfer the fermented cider—and not the lees—from the first carboy to the second carboy.

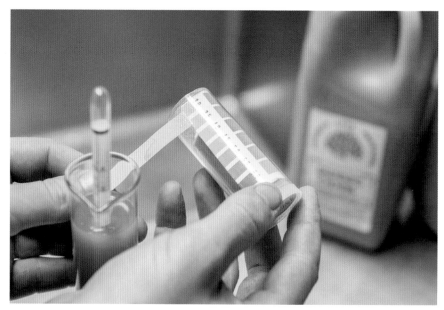
Use narrow-range litmus paper to measure pH.

Thermometer

All you need is an inexpensive glass lab thermometer. You need an accurate temperature reading at several steps in the cidermaking process, but there's no need to measure the temperature to the decimal place, so you don't need a fancy electronic thermometer.

Narrow-Range Litmus Paper

Measuring the pH—or acidity—of your juice is an important part of the cidermaking process, but you don't need to buy a pH meter. A pH meter can be expensive and require maintenance and calibration. Simple, inexpensive, narrow-range litmus paper will measure the pH effectively. Look for litmus paper that focuses as closely as possible on pH between 3 and 4.5. Litmus paper that measures a large range won't be sensitive enough to allow for an accurate reading.

Hydrometer and Cylinder

A hydrometer and a graduated cylinder are essential to measuring the amount of fermentable sugar in the juice. The best source for an inexpensive hydrometer and cylinder is a home winemaking supplier. When selecting a hydrometer, you want to look at the measurement scale. Some will measure specific gravity, others will measure brix, and still others will measure both. These are just different scales—like Fahrenheit versus Celsius—for measuring the same thing. If your hydrometer measures in one scale and your cider books explain the process in another, you have some math to do. In this book we use specific gravity.

Other Equipment

There are some simple household items that will make the cidermaking process easier for you: a plastic milk crate and a clear plastic jug. A milk crate is typically the right size to hold a glass carboy. Place the carboy in the crate to make it easier to carry and to prevent it from banging against anything, such as a concrete cellar floor. A clear plastic or glass jug will be helpful when transferring the juice and cider between containers.

When you are ready to bottle your cider, you will also need bottles—this can be anything from beer or wine bottles to growlers—and something to seal them with.

INGREDIENTS

Apples are the most important ingredient in your cider (see chapter 3)—but sulfur dioxide, yeast and, optionally, yeast nutrients, will improve the final product.

Sulfur Dioxide

Sulfur dioxide, also known by its chemical formula SO2, is used in cidermaking as an antimicrobial agent and an antioxidant. It is typically added twice in the cidermaking process: first, before the yeast is added to discourage the development of undesirable yeast or other organisms, and later, when the fermentation is complete to prevent oxidation and malolactic fermentation.

The practice of using sulfur dates back centuries, when sulfur was burned in cider barrels. Today, Campden tablets, which are made of potassium metabisulfite, are used by home cidermakers to add sulfur dioxide to the cider. They can be purchased from a home winemaking supplier.

Yeast

Yeast is essential to the fermentation process. Without it, your juice will never become cider. Although some cidermakers rely on natural fermentation—utilizing the yeasts on the apple skins or in the air and on the surfaces of the cider room—it can be an unreliable method, especially for the novice cidermaker. Most cidermakers choose to treat their juice with sulfur dioxide to eliminate the natural yeast, and then inoculate with a yeast specifically designed for making cider or wine. The best yeasts for cidermaking are tolerant of sulfur dioxide, forgiving of minor temperature changes, and proven to be strong enough to ferment the cider to full dryness.

There are numerous options when it comes to yeast. Each experienced cidermaker swears by a different strain or brand—or several yeasts combined—an allegiance that comes after much experimentation. Some yeasts impart specific flavors or other characteristics to the cider, but for the purposes of your first batch of cider, choose a strong yeast that ferments cleanly, allowing the flavors of the apples to shape the cider. Farnum Hill Ciders are made using Lalvin DV10 and Red Star Pasteur Champagne yeast (which, despite its name, is not for making sparkling wines). Both are known for strong fermentations, even in less-than-ideal circumstances, and they have neutral effects on the flavor and aroma of the finished cider. These yeasts are available from winemaking suppliers.

Yeast Nutrients

It is not essential to add yeast nutrients, but they can contribute to a healthy, strong fermentation, which is the best defense against the development of unpleasant aromas and flavors. The yeast is gobbling up the sugar in the juice and converting it to alcohol and carbon dioxide, but yeast needs other nutrients, such as nitrogen and thiamine, to remain healthy. You can use any brand of yeast nutrient you find at winemaking and home brewing suppliers.

BEST PRACTICES FOR SANITATION

Cleanliness is important, but maintaining your cidermaking equipment isn't difficult. Hot water is the number one option for cleaning your tools. (Don't use scented detergents.) There are other solvents available, but they are rarely necessary. If you do choose to clean with something such as sodium percarbonate, soda ash, or caustic soda, follow the package directions and safety precautions carefully. The best rule of thumb is to do the best cleaning job you can without going overboard. Sight and smell will typically tell you if you've done a thorough job or not.

Cleaning a Carboy

A carboy, with its narrow mouth, can be the most difficult piece of cidermaking equipment to clean. A glass carboy makes your job easier because smooth glass is easier to clean and because you can see the inside surfaces of the container. As with all of your cidermaking tools, hot water is typically sufficient for cleaning, unless your inspection of the container reveals something especially gross.

Use a flexible brush to clean the carboy.

A flexible carboy brush can be helpful in cleaning every surface of the carboy with hot water. A bottle-washing attachment for your sink is another option. Often sold by home brewing suppliers, this tool directs a jet of hot water into the bottle or carboy.

A Commercial Cider Room

We store and pack apples and make cider in barns that were originally built for cows and milk. The first of them was built in the late-eighteenth century. In the early 1980s, after years of adapting our work to the buildings, we began to adapt the buildings to accommodate our work. We poured concrete, raised ceilings, moved buildings, all in the effort to pack and store apples and make a little sweet cider on the side. Oops.

By the mid-'90s, we had begun to get more serious about real cider and less hopeful about packing apples. The buildings we'd rejiggered for handling apples were all wrong again when it came to cidermaking—small floor drains, perfectly flat floors, high ceilings (for stacking apple bins 22 feet [6.7 m] high), and no provision for warming or cooling large volumes of liquid or getting water quickly to an indoor drain. We became squeegee masters.

Every cidermaker deals with some version of our problems: temperature, space, and water.

The other day it was 18 degrees below zero (-28°C) here in northern New Hampshire. We couldn't clean barrels on the loading dock or do anything else with liquid out of doors. The heated area of our barns is too crowded with tanks and barrels to wash indoors, and we'd never get the rinse water across our flat floors to our tiny drains anyway. We had to wait for a warmer day to work with the barrels.

It's a good thing we like the results of slow, cool fermentations, because I'm not sure what we'd do if we didn't. We use yeast that ferments reliably to dryness regardless of the cold. We work around the frigid days, and choose warmer (above freezing) days to do our outdoor winter cider work. In the summer, we scramble in the other direction, keeping the cider cool in our apple storages and only working outside when it's not brutally hot.

I guess it works out—we're usually pleased by our ciders.

We're thinking of putting up a building designed for cidermaking, but in the meanwhile, we'll work with what we have.

5

Your First Batch of Cider

While the fall is often thought of as cidermaking season, you can start your cider project any time you have all the necessary ingredients and equipment on hand, a warm space for starting fermentation, and a cool place for storing the cider during fermentation. (See chapter 4.)

The method outlined in this chapter is the one used to produce Farnum Hill's still cider. The whole process will take about one month—or longer if you choose to let your first batch of cider mature.

As always, it begins with the apples. Find the best fresh, sweet, pure apple juice you can buy, and get started. See page 67 for more information on finding high-quality apple juice.

Timeline for First-Batch

In Advance

- Purchase the necessary equipment and ingredients.

Day 1

- Purchase the best apple juice you can, transfer it to the carboy, and add sulfur dioxide.
- Taste the juice and test the pH and specific gravity.

Day 2

- Pitch the yeast and place the open carboy in a warm space.

About Day 3 to Day 7

- Wait and watch as the fermentation process begins.
- When fermentation is underway, move the open carboy to a cool space.

About Week 2

- Add the bored bung when any frothing has stopped.
- Add the airlock when fermentation is less vigorous.
- Add yeast nutrients, if using.

About Week 2 to Week 4

- Wait and watch as the fermentation process slows.
- Test the pH of the cider.
- Continue to wait until fermentation stops and sediment falls out of the cider.
- Rack the cider and add sulphur dioxide.

Month 2 and Beyond

- Let the cider mature.
- Bottle the cider.

ADDING SULFUR DIOXIDE

As soon as you get your juice into the carboy, you should add sulfur dioxide (SO2) most likely in the form of Campden tablets. At this point in the process, sulfur dioxide acts primarily as an antimicrobial agent, suppressing unwanted yeasts and other organisms in preparation for your addition of yeast. Follow the instructions on the Campden tablets package to add 50 parts per million of sulfur dioxide to the juice.

Wait twenty-four hours before pitching the yeast. This ensures that the sulfur dioxide has time to disperse and do its work. You may see the juice lighten somewhat in color during this waiting period, because sulfur dioxide also helps to prevent oxidation.

Add sulfur dioxide to juice as an antimicrobial agent.

TESTING

It is helpful to know the pH and specific gravity of the juice you are starting with to give yourself a better understanding of the cider you are making. You also want to taste the juice and record your tasting notes, so you can assess how those flavors and characteristics change in the cider-making process. (See chapter 2.)

Following the instructions on the package of the litmus paper, test and record the pH of the juice. A juice's pH is a measure of the strength of the juice's acidity. You are looking for a pH below 3.7, which is acidic enough to

prevent the growth of many microbes and allow for the effective use of sulfur dioxide in the form of Campden tablets, another antimicrobial measure.

Measure the temperature of the juice, and then, following the package instructions for the hydrometer, test and record the specific gravity of the juice. The hydrometer measures the soluble solids in the juice, essentially measuring its fermentable sugar. The specific gravity of the juice will give you a sense of the amount of alcohol that will be present in the finished cider.

CIDERMAKING TIP

Specific Gravity and Potential Alcohol

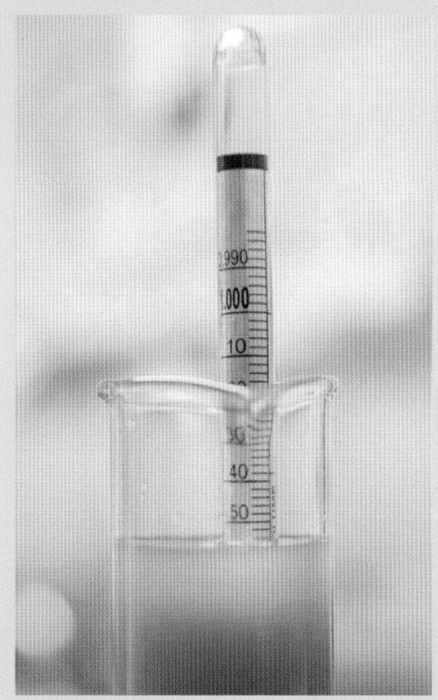

Specific Gravity of Juice (S.G.)	Potential Alcohol by Volume of Cider (ABV)
1.040	5.1
1.045	5.8
1.050	6.5
1.055	7.2
1.060	7.8
1.065	8.6
1.070	9.2
1.075	9.9
1.080	10.6
1.085	11.3
1.090	12

PITCHING THE YEAST

Begin by removing about one gallon (4 L) of the juice from the carboy into a clean jug or other convenient container.

Following the package instructions, hydrate the yeast in a container of warm water, stirring to combine, and let the mixture stand for twenty minutes to proof. The yeast will be frothing. Then feed the yeast with a small amount of juice from the gallon jug and allow it to continue to froth for about ten more minutes. This step makes the yeast stronger and may acclimate it to the sulfur dioxide present. Pour the frothing yeast mixture into the carboy, making sure you get all the yeast into the carboy. Rinse the yeast container with some juice from the gallon (4 L) jug into the carboy. Then return enough of the remaining juice to the carboy to leave a small amount of headspace below the neck.

Place the open carboy—without a bung or airlock—in a warm place to encourage fermentation. The ideal temperature is a consistent 65°F to 70°F (18°C to 21°C). Placing the carboy in a sturdy milk crate is a good idea because you will move it during the fermentation process; the milk crate will make the carboy easier to carry. As fermentation progresses, the carboy may expel a frothy mixture that will drip down the sides of the container. A cookie sheet or tray under the carboy will protect the floor or furniture.

WAITING

Fermentation will start slowly. You can check on the process each day to watch the progress. At first, it will look like nothing is happening. Then small bubbles will appear. Then the juice will begin bubbling vigorously and may spew froth out of the mouth of the carboy. This can take several days or as long as a week, depending on factors such as the temperature. If the carboy is frothing, you can use a wet cloth to clean the outside of the container. Don't use soap or other cleaning agents that could contaminate the cider. Otherwise, leave the carboy undisturbed.

Pitching the yeast

MOVING THE CARBOY

When vigorous fermentation is underway, you should move the carboy to a cooler place if available. The ideal temperature is a consistent 40°F to 60°F (4°C to 16°C). At this point in the process, you must be careful not to introduce air into the cider. Move the carboy with a minimal amount of sloshing or agitation.

ADDING THE BORED BUNG

The carboy is still open. It needs to remain open until the fermentation has slowed—you'll see strong streams of bubbles, but any frothing will have stopped. If you put the bung in before fermentation has slowed, the pressure building up inside the carboy will, at best, expel it. At worst, it will shatter the carboy. When the fermentation has slowed down, place the bored bung loosely in the mouth of the carboy. Don't add the airlock yet. The bung is a test. If, after a day, the bung remains in place without any frothing, you can push the bung fully into the mouth. If the bung is soon expelled or covered in froth, remove the bung, clean it, and wait a day to try again.

Insert the bored bung when fermentation has slowed.

ADDING THE AIRLOCK

Two common types of bored bungs and airlocks

Add the airlock to prevent oxidation.

After you have secured the bored bung, wait a day before adding the airlock. The fermentation process is still producing enough carbon dioxide to create positive pressure and prevent damaging air from entering the carboy through the hole in the bung.

When you are ready to add the airlock, add water to the airlock and insert it into the bung. If the bubbles are rising rapidly in the airlock, remove it. It's too soon. You can test the airlock again the next day. If the bubbles are regular but not rapid, leave the airlock in place.

FEEDING THE YEAST

At this stage, you can consider feeding the yeast a bit. Use the minimum amount (or even less) that the package recommends and follow the instructions for adding the nutrients to the carboy. The key is to add the nutrients to the fermenting liquid very slowly. The nutrients are more soluble than carbon dioxide and will drive some of the carbon dioxide out of solution in your carboy. If you just dump the nutrients in, expect a frothy volcano and be ready to mop your floor. If you add it gently and slowly, expect to see the liquid get a bit excited, then settle back down to a happy fermentation. When it has, replace the airlock.

WAITING

Once the airlock is in place, you should leave the fermenting cider undisturbed. Just watch the progress. You will see the rapid fermentation slow and then, over the course of several weeks, come to a near stop.

Lees, which is made up of solids from the juice and expired yeast, will have built up at the bottom of the carboy during the fermentation process. Even after the fermentation has finished, the lees will continue to fall to the bottom and the cider will become clearer.

TESTING

When the fermentation has nearly stopped and you see only the occasional rising bubbles, it's time to test the cider.

Working quickly to minimize the cider's exposure to air, remove the bung and airlock from the carboy and start by smelling the cider. The cider should smell pleasant. If you detect rotten eggs, compost, decay, cabbage, or garlic, your cider may be in trouble. (See chapter 6 for some potential solutions.)

Use the plastic tubing to siphon a small amount of the cider for your evaluation. Taste it. It may taste a little harsh. That's fine. The flavor typically mellows as the cider matures. Then, using the litmus paper, test the pH of the cider. The pH level will have risen some during the fermentation process, but that change will not be clearly detectable on narrow-range litmus paper. (If it is noticeable, see chapter 6.) You can also test the specific gravity using the hydrometer to confirm that the fermentation is completed. Fully fermented cider will have a specific gravity of 1.00 or lower.

Replace the bung and airlock and wait until fermentation has stopped completely.

CIDERMAKING TIP

Equipment for Racking

- Full carboy
- Campden tablets
- Empty carboy
- Plastic tubing
- Utility tape
- Scissors
- Glass for your first taste of cider
- Extra clean container for excess cider
- Dry cider, neutral white wine, or distilled water, as needed
- Solid carboy bung

RACKING

When there are no bubbles visible, fermentation has stopped completely.

If all has gone well with the fermentation—there were no unpleasant odors or a dramatic increase in pH when you tested—you can leave the cider on its lees for a week or two without seeing any change beyond increasing clarity. If these flaws are apparent, see chapter 6 for some potential solutions. More time on the lees could exacerbate the problems.

"Racking" is simply transferring the cider from the carboy in which it fermented into the second carboy, where it will mature. You'll do this by siphoning the cider through the plastic tubing, leaving the lees behind. This is also the time to add more sulfur dioxide, this time primarily to prevent oxidation and malolactic fermentation (in which a bacteria converts malic acid to lactic acid) or other bacterial activity.

Read these instructions for racking carefully and collect all the necessary equipment before beginning the process. It is important to work efficiently to minimize the amount of time that the cider is in contact with the air.

Begin by moving the full carboy to a table, being careful not to agitate the liquid and disperse the lees. The full carboy needs to be at a higher level than the second, receiving carboy to siphon the liquid. Allow the full carboy to sit undisturbed for twenty-four hours so the lees can settle after the move.

When you are ready to rack, place the empty carboy near and below the full carboy. Follow the instructions on the package of the Campden tablets to prepare 30 to 35 parts per million of sulfur dioxide, which will be added later in the racking process.

Remove the bung and airlock from the full carboy and lower the plastic tubing into the cider until it is an inch (2.5 cm) above the lees, with the mouth of the tubing against the side of the carboy. You can secure the tubing in place at the neck of the carboy with utility tape to prevent it from dropping into the lees. It's important not to disturb the lees, which will make the cider cloudy again.

Place the other end of the plastic tubing near the empty carboy and use your mouth to create suction, drawing the cider into the tubing. As the cider begins to flow, siphon a small amount of cider into a glass and then insert the tube into the receiving carboy, resting the mouth of the tubing at the bottom of the container to minimize the amount of air introduced into the mixture. (Some unwanted aromas can be treated with a "splashy" racking, which intentionally introduces air. See chapter 6.)

When the receiving carboy is about half full, add the prepared Campden tablets.

Be cautious again when you near the end of the siphoning process. You don't want the receiving carboy to overflow, so have an extra clean container on hand for excess cider. And you don't want to suck lees or air into the carboy. Leave some cider behind if necessary.

You need to fill the receiving carboy completely, into the neck and within a half-inch (1.3 cm) of the bung, to reduce the surface exposed to the air. You will likely have more than enough cider, but if you don't you can use dry cider, neutral white wine, or even water to top off the carboy.

Close the full carboy with a solid bung.

To rack, place the full carboy on a table.

Place the empty, smaller carboy at a lower level.

Lower the plastic tubing into the full carboy, with the mouth of the tubing against the side.

Use your mouth to create suction. Place the end of the plastic tubing in the empty, smaller carboy.

Siphon the cider into the smaller carboy. Have an extra container available for any excess cider.

If necessary, top off the carboy with dry cider, neutral white wine, or water before adding the bung.

TASTING

This is your first taste of your first batch of cider. The first question is: Do you like it? Now taste the cider the same way you tasted the juice, making notes about the aromas, flavors, and other characteristics you detect in the cider. (See chapter 2.)

If you love the cider and want to drink it now, it's time to bottle it. But most ciders made from tannic and acidic apples benefit from some time to mature. Your cider will change over time, and those changes are more reliable and positive in a larger container than in a smaller container. (If you find off-aromas or other flaws in the cider, see chapter 6 to diagnose the problem and find troubleshooting techniques.)

MATURING

If you've chosen to mature your cider, you can taste the change over weeks or months or even years. Wait a month between tastings. (Always top the cider off with dry cider, neutral white wine, or water to fill the carboy after tasting.) Typically, over time, the tannins in the cider round out, becoming less astringent, and acids soften, becoming less harsh. Often as these changes occur, other attractive aromas and flavors develop.

Store the cider in a cool place as it matures. Leave it undisturbed.

BOTTLING

The bottling process is very similar to the racking process. If you've allowed the cider to mature, you may find a thin layer of lees at the bottom of the carboy. Follow the same procedure of inserting the tubing and siphoning the cider into the selected bottles. The key here is to fill the containers completely and seal them tightly.

Congratulations! You've completed your first batch of cider. Enjoy it.

Our First Ciders

In the days when we were growers, packers, and shippers of McIntosh, Cortland, and Red and Golden Delicious, and Farnum Hill Ciders didn't even exist, we often put a barrel of cider down to ferment. We did it the way other folks in New England did in those days—we filled a used whiskey barrel with indifferent sweet cider, added a few raisins and some brown sugar, put the barrel somewhere it wouldn't freeze, and made an airlock with a bung, some wax, a piece of fuel line, and a jug of water. Sometimes it froze, and sometimes it didn't. So sometimes we made rough hard cider, and other times we inadvertently made apple booze. We usually bottled it in late winter or early spring. It was fun and made for rowdy parties, but was always a reliable headache in a glass.

But, when we started grubbing out our old dessert orchards and replanting them with real cider fruit, we had to get serious about learning to make good cider. We knew we wanted it to be delicious and to reflect the fruit and the land where it grew, but we didn't know much else. We studied all we could find on the subject, in the United States and in Europe. When our orchards finally started to produce a few good cider apples, we filled dozens of carboys and fermented them wherever we could (a walk-in cooler in the barn, the basement of a house, and so on). We made hundreds of gallons of perfectly horrid stuff.

We had unfathomable (to us) fermentation problems, yeast problems, acidity problems, and all manner of other problems, producing a lot of cider that took a lot of self-delusion to like. The main thing we learned in those days was that it's very easy to persuade yourself that the cider you've worked so hard to make *must* be delicious and to try to choke it down, but that if it's really worse than a cheap six pack or jug of wine, you should probably admit the truth, dump out the cider, find something else to drink, and try again. That's as true today as it was then.

Happily, after a few years, we began to get the hang of it (with generous help from cidermakers and winemakers around the world). A couple of barrels even tasted genuinely good to us. In 1995, we finally became a bonded winery and started selling a few cases of cider. The cider we sold in those first years wouldn't stand up to our standards today. We didn't yet know what sort of cider we wanted to (or were able to) make from these unfamiliar apples, but at least those early ciders had pleasing bittersweet character and good acid and fruit.

We've learned a lot since we put those first carboys in our basement. There's no reason for you to wander through the same tortuous learning adventure. If you follow the directions in this chapter, your first carboy will be a thousand times better than our first ones were.

Your Second Batch of Cider

If your first batch was delicious, drink it! Then follow your notes and the steps in chapter 5 again and see if you can replicate the results. Take thorough notes with each batch. There are innumerable variables when it comes to cidermaking—some that you can control and some that you can't—and the best cidermakers are careful observers who practice their cidermaking skills with batch after batch.

If your first batch didn't please you, ask yourself, "Why?" Perhaps the cider is flawed, or perhaps you made a good cider that simply isn't your idea of what "good" cider should taste like.

For the small-batch home cidermaker, there are three much-feared flaws: the presence of excess hydrogen sulfide, which can smell of rotten eggs or cabbage and garlic; unintentional malolactic fermentation, which dulls the acids in the cider; and acetic fermentation, which turns your cider into cider vinegar.

It's important to note that these "common" flaws are not all that common. Don't be in a hurry to diagnose one or the other during the fermentation process or at racking. Don't overreact at the slightest aroma coming from your carboy. If the evidence of one of these flaws is clear, however, there may be steps you can take to correct them—or, if the cider is too flawed, to learn from the mistake and start fermenting your next batch of cider.

There are other, even less common flaws, such as mousiness (the presence of a strong, mouse-like smell), from which there is no reasonable rescue—except another batch of cider.

When acting to remedy a perceived flaw, remember that every action you take to correct a flaw can have other, unintended consequences on the cider. Sometimes the best course of action is to learn to love your flawed cider, or pour it out and start again.

 CIDERMAKING TIP

The Big Three

These three flaws, though not common in home cidermaking, are of concerned conversation among home cidermakers.

Excess Hydrogen Sulfide

Produces: An unpleasant aroma of rotten eggs

Caused by: Sulfur compounds in the fruit at pressing, stress on the yeast, autolyzing yeast

Occurs: At any point before racking

Diagnosed by: Smell, during fermentation or at racking

Corrected with: Yeast nutrients during fermentation, splashy racking, copper pennies

Prevented by: Healthy yeast environment, less time on the lees

Unintended Malolactic Fermentation

Produces: Cider without noticeable acid

Caused by: Lactobacillus and other bacteria

Occurs: During or after alcoholic fermentation

Diagnosed by: Sight, after the completion of alcoholic fermentation, or smell and taste, during racking or maturing

Corrected with: Immediate racking, addition of sulfur dioxide, and storage at a cool temperature if diagnosed at the start of malolactic fermentation; with the addition of purchased acid or the use of the cider for blending with a more acidic cider if malolactic fermentation has already occurred.

Prevented by: Early racking, addition of sulfur dioxide immediately after fermentation and storage at a cool temperature or the addition of sulfur dioxide before racking while the cider is on the lees

Acetic Fermentation

Produces: Apple cider vinegar

Caused by: Acetobacter bacteria

Occurs: During or after alcoholic fermentation

Diagnosed by: Smell, during the alcoholic fermentation, or taste, during racking or maturing

Corrected with: Acetic fermentation cannot be corrected, but you can make delicious apple cider vinegar

Prevented by: Clean equipment, efforts to prevent juice and cider from exposure to oxygen, storage at a cool temperature

EXCESS HYDROGEN SULFIDE (H2S)

Hydrogen sulfide is a compound that gives cider the unpleasant aroma of rotten eggs.

There are three main culprits in the production of excess hydrogen sulfide. Sulfur compounds may have been present on the apples and transferred to the juice at pressing. (Some common fungicides used in orchards, even when applied following best practices, can leave a residue of sulfur compounds.) The yeast may have struggled to get the necessary sugar and additional nutrients it needed during fermentation or have been otherwise stressed, which can cause the production of excess hydrogen sulfide and other off-gases. Or excess hydrogen sulfide may have been produced by autolyzing (decomposing) yeast while the cider sat on the lees awaiting racking.

Diagnosing

The presence of excess hydrogen sulfide gas can be diagnosed during fermentation or at racking. It is diagnosed by nose. Excess hydrogen sulfide produces a strong smell that is often compared to rotten eggs. Hydrogen sulfide is a normal by-product of yeast metabolism and will always be produced in a small amount during fermentation. Very low levels of hydrogen sulfide can contribute to the cider's pleasing complexity. However, if the levels are excessive the cider will just smell plain bad.

Smell the fermenting cider during fermentation to diagnose some potential flaws.

The causes of excess hydrogen sulfide production during fermentation are not completely understood, but many factors contribute including low levels of nutrients for the yeast, the use of sulfur in the orchard, and high levels of suspended solids in the juice. If present in strong concentration, it can develop into compounds that smell of cabbage or garlic or even compost and sewage. The human nose is extremely sensitive to all these compounds. However, the human brain is easily fooled by expectation and fear. If you expect to smell these aromas near the airlock or in the tasting glass, you may convince yourself that you do. Asking another person to smell and describe the aromas coming from the airlock or the tasting glass, without offering your own descriptions, is one way to double-check your impressions.

Correcting

If you confidently diagnose the presence of excess hydrogen sulfide during fermentation, it's time to feed the yeast. Yeast nutrients are available from winemaking and home brewing suppliers. Follow the directions in chapter 5 to feed the yeast.

If excess hydrogen sulfide is present at the time of racking, there are two potential remedies that make sense for the small-batch home cidermaker. These remedies are more effective if the scent is on the "rotten egg" end of the spectrum than they are if the scent is on the far more concentrated "compost" end. The first takes place during racking.

In the typical racking process, every precaution is taken to limit the amount of air the cider is exposed to when it is siphoned from one carboy to another. The opposite is true if excess hydrogen sulfide is present. Instead of lowering the plastic tubing to the bottom of the receiving carboy, you will position the plastic tubing near the neck for a "splashy racking." A "splashy racking," as the name implies, splashes the cider into the receiving carboy, which can blow off the hydrogen sulfide.

Splashy racking is often effective in reducing hydrogen sulfide. You'll smell the difference immediately near the neck of the carboy or in the tasting glass. But splashy racking also introduces oxygen into the cider, which can change the cider's flavors or exacerbate other flaws that are present, and it can blow off other, desirable aromas. If you do a "splashy racking," it's doubly important to add sulfur dioxide, in the form of Campden tablets, at this stage. (See chapter 5.) Sulfur dioxide will help prevent excessive oxidation of the cider.

The second potential remedy is employed after racking. It can be used in conjunction with a splashy racking, but if the splashy racking was ineffective, your cider may be beyond remedy. For this hydrogen sulfide solution, you will need clean pennies made before 1982. Before 1982, the penny was made of pure copper. Copper reacts with the hydrogen sulfide and eliminates it.

Experiment first in your tasting glass. Sniff the cider. If you smell rotten eggs, drop a penny into the cider. Swirl the glass and then blow to remove any lingering aromas. Sniff the cider again. If a small amount of hydrogen sulfide was present, it should be gone. You can take this same approach with your carboy, adding a small handful of clean, copper pennies to remove the hydrogen sulfide.

In a commercial cidery with hundreds of gallons—and thousands of dollars—at stake, there are more extreme measures available, such as the addition of copper sulfate and ascorbic acid, but for the home cidermaker, dealing with just a few gallons, these treatments are overly elaborate.

Preventing

For home cidermakers who are not growing and pressing their own apples, it can be impossible to control the presence of sulfur compounds in the juice at the start of the fermentation process. The cidermaker can, however, work to provide a hospitable environment for the yeast, preventing the stress that can produce excess hydrogen sulfide by following the advice in chapter 4 and chapter 5, including choosing a strong yeast, adding the recommended amount of sulfur dioxide before fermentation, proofing the yeast properly before pitching it, and feeding the yeast as the fermentation settles down.

At the end of fermentation, hydrogen sulfide production by autolyzing yeast can be prevented by limiting the amount of time that the cider sits on the lees. This is a balancing act, because time on the lees can also improve the clarity and complexity of a cider. However, if a cider smells of rotten eggs at the end of the fermentation process, or a cider that did not have an aroma of rotten eggs at the end of the fermentation process begins to acquire one as it sits on the lees, it should be racked immediately.

UNINTENDED MALOLACTIC FERMENTATION

During malolactic fermentation, malic acid is transformed into lactic acid. Because malic acid is a strong, sharp, bright acid and lactic acid is a weaker, broad and duller acid, the result of malolactic fermentation is a bigger, richer, fatter sensation in the mouth.

In some wines—for example, many New World chardonnays—malolactic fermentation is an intended process. Grapes contain several different types of acid, so the malolactic fermentation creates a full mouthfeel by converting the malic acid without eliminating the dominant tartaric acid and the other acids that give the wine its balancing acidity.

Apples, however, contain primarily malic acid, so malolactic fermentation in cider production most often produces a dull, unbalanced cider.

Unintended malolactic fermentation is caused by lactobacilli, bacteria that are also used in the production of cheese, pickles, and other foods. Some winemakers inoculate their wines with bacteria that causes malolactic fermentation. Most cidermakers work hard to avoid it.

Diagnosing

The odds that your cider room has been infected with a lactobacillus are low, but if the bacteria are present, malolactic fermentation can occur during or after the alcoholic fermentation. It can be diagnosed at the end of the alcoholic fermentation or during racking.

If, after the alcoholic fermentation has completely stopped, the cider begins to bubble again, it is most likely undergoing malolactic fermentation, which can progress very quickly.

At racking or during subsequent tastings if you allow the cider to mature, you can detect malolactic fermentation by mouth. Has the cider lost palpable acidity? In your tasting notes, did you describe the cider as having a big, full mouthfeel, and stewed or very ripe fruits and earthy flavors? These are indications of a malolactic fermentation. During malolactic fermentation, you will also see a rapid rise in the pH level as the acid is converted.

Correcting

Many common strains of lactobacillus are sensitive to sulfur dioxide and temperature fluctuations.

If you diagnose malolactic fermentation in progress by sight (through rising bubbles) as the finished cider sits on its lees awaiting racking, rack the cider immediately. The addition of sulfur dioxide during the racking process will retard or stop the malolactic fermentation process. Store the racked cider below 60°F (16°C) to further reduce the chances of continued malolactic fermentation.

If malolactic fermentation has already occurred when you diagnose it, there are several options.

Some cidermakers choose to add malic acid to replace the bright acidity which is lost during malolactic fermentation. Other acids, such as tartaric or citric or an acid blend, can also be added to cider that has undergone malolactic fermentation. These acids are typically available from a winemaking or home brewing supplier. Unfortunately, these purchased acids can impart an intense, artificial-tasting sharpness, similar to that found in tart candies. If you choose to use additional acid, follow the package instructions, starting with the smallest dose.

Other cidermakers will keep the finished cider for blending with another batch. (See chapter 7.) The full mouthfeel of the cider that underwent malolactic fermentation could be the perfect balance for a sharper, thinner cider produced in another carboy.

Most cidermakers, though, will just enjoy their cider. Cider that has undergone malolactic fermentation is not, perhaps, what you were hoping

Add sulfur dioxide at racking to help prevent some potential flaws.

to make, but the flavors that develop are far different from those of batches not exposed to lactobacillus. The bright, tropical, and citrus descriptions that usually fill your tasting notes will likely be replaced with stewed fruits and woody flavors.

Preventing

If you've never had a batch of cider undergo malolactic fermentation and you have no reason to believe that your cider room hosts lactobacillus, there is no reason to take preventive measures. Unintended malolactic fermentation is rare in home cidermaking.

If, however, you have been in the minority of home cidermakers who have been victim of unintended malolactic fermentation, you can reduce the chances of a reoccurrence by following many of the same steps that you would take to halt a malolactic fermentation you diagnosed before racking.

Racking soon after the end of the alcoholic fermentation, adding sulfur dioxide as recommended during the typical racking process, and storing the racked cider below 60°F (16°C) will help to prevent malolactic fermentation. If you wish to leave the cider on the lees for a longer period of time before racking to allow the cider to drop bright and develop additional flavors, you can reduce the chances of malolactic fermentation by adding sulfur dioxide at this point, instead of waiting for the racking process. Follow the instructions on the package of the Campden tablets to prepare and add 30 to 35 parts per million of sulfur dioxide.

ACETIC FERMENTATION

Acetic fermentation is the process through which alcohol is converted into acetic acid, the distinctive component in vinegar. Acetic fermentation occurs when a strain of acetobacter bacteria is present and the cider is exposed to oxygen and moderate temperatures.

Diagnosing

Acetic fermentation can occur during or after alcoholic fermentation. It can be recognized by smell during the alcoholic fermentation or by taste during or after racking. Cidermakers often recognize the presence of acetic acid by the "catching" sensation the sourness of vinegar causes at the back of the throat as you swallow the cider.

Correcting

If acetic fermentation has occurred or is underway, there is no way to reverse the process. You are now making apple cider vinegar.

You can encourage the acetic fermentation by exposing the cider to more oxygen. Unlike the cidermaking process, the vinegar making process thrives on oxygen. Transfer the liquid to an open container and stir once a day to promote acetic fermentation. Temperature also affects acetic fermentation. Store the liquid between 60°F to 80°F (16°C to 27°C).

The acetic fermentation process will take three to four weeks. Taste the developing vinegar until it reaches the desire strength. During the vinegar making process, a vinegar "mother" may form. This jellylike substance or film is a collection of cellulose and acetobacter. It is harmless and can be strained out to halt acetic fermentation. It can also be reserved to inoculate future batches of vinegar.

Preventing

Acetic fermentation requires the presence of acetobacter and oxygen and a moderate temperature.

To prevent acetic fermentation in future batches, be sure you clean all the necessary equipment before starting alcoholic fermentation to prevent the introduction of acetobacter. Each step you take to avoid exposing the juice or cider to oxygen also reduces the chances of acetic fermentation. Adding sulfur dioxide to the juice, using an airlock, racking carefully, and topping off the racked carboy are all steps in the cidermaking process that also prevent acetic fermentation. Storing your cider at below 60°F (16°C) is also a smart preventive measure.

OTHER POTENTIAL FLAWS

Some far less common flaws include the following:

Mousiness

A little-understood flaw, mousiness is easily detected in tasting. It is most frequently described as the aroma of mouse droppings, although some people perceive it as bread-like. It is thought to be caused by slow-developing strains of lactobacillus or brettanomyces bacteria. The defect typically arises during storage. It can't be corrected.

Discoloration

Exposure to oxygen is the most common culprit when your cider changes color. Oxygen will give most cider a brown tone, much like an apple bitten and exposed to air. To avoid this, take all precautions to limit exposure to oxygen.

Exposure to metal during the pressing process, far rarer, can also cause a change in cider color. If the juice was exposed to iron or copper, the cider can take on a black or green hue. This discoloration is most likely to occur when cider is exposed to air after bottling. You can use citric acid to test if metal is the cause. Divide the bottle into two glasses and add a pinch of citric acid to one. If the glass with citric acid changes color significantly more slowly, metal exposure is likely the cause. Although there are techniques used at the commercial scale to remediate the cider, for the home brewer there is little recourse.

Haze

A cider that hasn't "dropped bright" before racking and bottling is said to have a "haze." This haze or sediment can be caused by microbes, pectin or, very rarely, a high level of tannins. If the cider tastes good, this is not usually a problem for home cidermakers. Bottle the cider while hazy or simply give the cider more time to drop bright.

Microbial haze can usually be avoided by good sanitation practices. Pectin haze can be prevented or partially remedied with a pectolytic enzyme. And tannic haze, the most rarely seen version, can sometimes be fined from cider using gelatin and bentonite available at a winemaking supplier. Be aware, however, that fining a tannin haze can remove the appealing structure of a cider.

"I DON'T LOVE IT."

This is the most common flaw with a home cidermaker's first batch of cider: Your cider doesn't have any major defects that render it undrinkable. You just didn't make a cider that is to your taste. Think about wine. Even wine lovers don't love every well-made wine they encounter. Each wine drinker has a preference for particular grapes or growing regions. It's similar with apples.

Don't worry if your first batch of cider isn't your ideal cider. It takes a lot of practice, a lot of trial and error, and a little luck to accomplish that.

Hopefully, you like the cider well enough to be proud of your efforts and to enjoy it. At the very least, you need to taste it, following the objective process outlined in chapter 2. What do you smell? What do you taste? How would you describe the mouthfeel? How would you describe the finish?

Now think about the cider subjectively. Which of those aromas, flavors, and sensations do you like? Which ones don't you like? Compare the tasting notes from your first batch of cider with your tasting notes for some ciders that you love. What do you feel is missing from your cider?

For the purposes of this exercise, your observations about acidity, bitterness, and astringency will be the most helpful. These three components can greatly affect how you feel about your first batch of cider. And they are the most easily manipulated in your next batch of cider through the apples you start with. Are you lacking the acidity that brings the cider to life in your mouth? Look for juice with more sharp apples for your next batch. Are you lacking the bitterness that balances acidity or the astringency that provides a solid structure for your cider? Look for juice with some bittersweet apples for your next batch.

The more nuanced flavor profile of a cider is more difficult to tailor. It takes time and tasting to learn which mix of apples (and even what growing environment in the orchard) will create the aromas of leather or stone fruit or moss you most prefer. Talk to experienced cidermakers and apple growers in your region for more guidance or, once you have more experience, experiment with post-fermentation blending. (See chapter 7.)

Don't Fear the Stink

At the cidery, we reckon our job is to let the apples make the cider, and try not to ruin it by our work. We try to keep our hands off the cider as much as we can, until it's ready to drink. That doesn't mean that we don't pay attention to the cider while it's fermenting and maturing—we pay constant attention—we just don't intervene any more than we absolutely need to. Once we've blended the apples, pressed them into juice, blended again and started fermentation, we try to leave things alone. We might feed the yeast a bit to keep the colony happy. When the cider drops bright, we'll rack it, to separate the lovely new cider from the lees. We taste and blend a bit at racking, but then we pull our hands away again.

If we smell something funky in the cider room, we chase it down. Nicole and I will smell our way around all of the tanks and barrels to discover the culprit. But we don't always do anything about it. We like faint funk in cider. If the cider is fermenting and starting to smell like rotten eggs, we reckon the yeast is unhappy, and we'll feed it a little. On very rare occasion, we might move it off its lees to another vessel. But we don't worry much about a little funk at the end of fermentation.

A lot of delicious food and drink has a bit of stink, along with other aromas. Think of Brie, or certain black olives, or good Châteauneuf-du-Pape—they all have a little bit of something that would be very unpleasant if they had a lot of it, but that's delightful in the little bit. Think of the agricultural countryside. The pleasant, reassuring aroma you smell is probably farmyard manure. Very nice during a walk on the hill, pretty nasty in the manure pit—it's all a matter of concentration.

I'm not sure how to describe the line we try not to let the cider cross. It's something like walking down the hill toward the manure pit: There's a moment when you've just gotten too close for pleasure. When we think we're getting too close, we do something about it if we can. We also really try to avoid malolactic fermentation, but we've blended some delicious ciders from batches that have snuck through unintended malolactic fermentation. We keep any ciders that have "gone wrong," until we need the tank or barrel again (unless we suspect they're harboring some horrible microbe). Then, if we haven't discovered a use for those ciders, they go down the drain. But we always learn from them, and quite often they prove useful in a blend.

Like good wine, good cider is pretty stable but constantly changing. It takes a fair bit of experience to even grasp the edge of understanding cider, and to learn how to work with the apples, the yeast, the containers, and the environment to produce a good one. To us, that's what makes cider cool.

CHAPTER 7

Your Third Batch of Cider and Beyond

The first lesson of cidermaking is that the apples make the cider. The second thing you learn is that good cidermaking is all about practice: learning to smell, taste, and see the cues that the developing cider is providing you, and how to respond (or not respond) to those signals. The first time you make a batch of cider, it will probably be good. The next time you follow that same process, drawing on your observations from the previous batches, it will probably be better and so on. So, don't be in a rush to move on from making the basic cider outlined in chapter 5. But when you feel accomplished at making a consistent cider, there's a whole world of cider to explore. At other respected cideries, cidermakers experiment with *méthode champenoise*, spontaneously fermented *cidre*, and ice cider. Other tools available to the cidermaker include blending cider, returning sugar, and introducing carbonation.

The other approaches to cidermaking outlined in this chapter have one thing in common with Farnum Hill Ciders' basic approach: The cider is an expression of the fruit. The processes are very different and the results of each process are unique, but the cidermakers featured here share a belief that cider starts with the apple and that the cidermaker's job is to intervene as little possible to turn the apple into a delicious fermented drink.

BLENDING

Commercial cideries often blend fermented ciders to create the finished product.

As discussed in previous chapters, commercial cideries rarely ferment a single apple variety in a batch, preferring to balance the cider's characteristics with the best qualities of different apples. Some cideries bottle directly from the tank when fermentation is complete; others blend finished ciders.

The blending process allows the cidermakers to adjust the aromas, tastes and sensations of the final product naturally. The home cidermaker who has several unbottled batches of fully fermented cider on hand can also experiment with blending.

The first step is tasting the ciders objectively, as outlined in chapter 2. When the tasting process is complete, consider your ideal cider. Does it have more or less acid? More or less bitterness? The goal of blending is to create something close to this ideal.

Now, identify the batch of cider that is most similar to your ideal. This will be your base; the other batches of cider will be used to add the other characteristics you desire. Perhaps you love the funky flavors of a cider that accidently went through malolactic fermentation, but wish it had an acidic component. If you have a more acidic batch available, you can add that.

Work in small batches. The results of blending can be surprising—and not always desirable. Take notes on the amount of each cider you add as you prepare each blend. Stir or swirl the blend gently, and allow it to sit for a few minutes to fully combine the liquids. Then taste the blends. Which is your favorite? When you've found a combination you love, use your notes to blend a full batch with the same ratios.

CARBONATION

Following the process outlined in chapter 5 produces a classic cider fermented to dryness. But sparkling cider is popular with many cider drinkers. One classic way to add bubbles to a fermented cider is through *méthode champenoise*, explained in the next section. However, this process, which involves a second fermentation in the bottle, also changes the cider in other ways.

A relatively simple process is used to add an effervescence to some still ciders without making additional changes to the flavors, aromas, and sensations of the cider. Carbon dioxide (CO_2) is slowly added to the cold cider in a steel tank.

The home cidermaker can experiment with carbonation using the following: a five-gallon (19 L) cornelius—or "corney"—keg with ball fittings, readily available from home brewing suppliers; compatible liquid and gas lines; and a carbon dioxide cylinder.

A cornelius keg is a steel cylinder with a removable lid (which allows for easy cleaning) designed to hold a liquid under pressure. There are two connections, one with a short tube to the top of the keg, and one with a longer tube to the bottom. Typically a cornelius keg is used to store and dispense a carbonated liquid, such as soda or beer. The liquid is dispensed from the bottom of the keg and an

To carbonate a still cider after racking, siphon the cider into a cornelius keg.

Trickle carbon dioxide into the cornelius keg while agitating.

Store carbonated cider in the cornelius keg.

inert gas is added to the top of the keg to maintain the pressure. Home cidermakers can add carbonation by attaching the gas line to the bottom of the keg instead. This allows the carbon dioxide to bubble up through the liquid. Over time, the carbon dioxide will be absorbed into the liquid, providing carbonation.

To carbonate your still cider, begin with cold liquid, which absorbs carbon dioxide more easily. Add the cider to the keg. Close the keg, being sure the gasket seals, and connect the gas line and carbon dioxide cylinder to the fitting reaching to the bottom of the keg. Let the carbon dioxide trickle into the keg for about 1 minute while agitating the keg. (If you are using a pressure gauge, look for 4 to 10 psi.) Continue agitating the keg for several minutes to aid carbon dioxide absorption, and allow it to sit for a day. Repeat the procedure on day two and day three. Adding the carbon dioxide over time produces fine bubbles, which most cidermakers prefer over large bubbles.

There are tools available to test the pressure of your keg, but the best approach is to evaluate the cider with your senses. Remove the gas line and replace it with the liquid line to sample a small amount of the cider. Does it have the amount of carbonation you prefer?

To dispense the sparkling cider into glasses, use the liquid line. If you plan to drink the cider over time, add the gas line to the top of the keg to introduce carbon dioxide above the liquid as you dispense it.

RETURNING SUGAR

Sugar can be reintroduced to a completely fermented, dry cider as is common in champagne production. Some cidermakers will choose to add unfermented apple juice to the completed cider, but the juice dramatically changes the flavor profile of the cider. Instead, at Poverty Lane Orchards, the cidermakers use small amounts of white sugar, as needed, to adjust a cider. The sugar has a more subtle effect than apple juice.

White sugar can be used to make a sweet cider or, as it is most often used at Poverty Lane Orchards, to bring out desirable fruit flavors that are muted in the dry cider.

There are also dangers associated with reintroducing sugar. The additional sugar can serve as food for any remaining yeast or other microbes. For this reason, only add sugar to fully dry ciders, store them at a low temperature, and use a cornelius keg instead of glass bottles. A cornelius keg is designed to withstand pressure that microbes can produce.

To return sugar to your cider, rack the cider into a cornelius keg. You can draw off some cider, as in blending, to experiment with, but the amounts of sugar you will add are so small as to make such small-scale experimentation difficult.

The amount of sugar to add is a matter of taste. About 10 grams of sugar per liter of liquid is returned to most brut champagnes. (The addition of sugar in Champagne production is called "dosage.") For the sweeter extra-dry Champagne, winemakers return up to 20 grams of sugar per liter. A noticeably sweet commercial cider may have as much as 40 grams of sugar per liter. At Poverty Lane Orchards, three to five grams of sugar are added per liter to produce its off-dry ciders.

Add the sugar, seal the cornelius keg, and store your cider at a cool temperature.

CIDERMAKING TIP

Equipment and Ingredients for Returning Sugar

- 5 gallons (19 L) still cider
- 5-gallon (19 L) cornelius keg with ball fittings
- Compatible liquid and gas lines
- Carbon dioxide cylinder
- White sugar
- Scale

MÉTHODE CHAMPENOISE

Méthode champenoise cider, so named for its use in Champagne production, uses a second, in-bottle fermentation to produce sparkling cider with delicate, persistent bubbles. The mouthfeel of a sparkling cider produced through this process will be different from one produced through carbonation. This is a low-tech way of creating bubbles, but disgorgement, one step in the process, does take some practice. Here, Autumn Stoscheck and Ezra Sherman of Eve's Cidery in the Finger Lakes region of New York share their well-practiced process for making *méthode champenoise* cider.

The process begins with the production of a fully dry still cider. A home cidermaker fermenting cider for this process should follow the steps in chapter 5, ensuring that the cider ferments completely, with one noticeable exception: In *méthode champenoise* production, you add less sulfur dioxide, in the form of Campden tablets, at racking. Because sulfur dioxide acts as an antimicrobial as well as an antioxidant, too much sulfur dioxide will create an inhospitable environment for the second fermentation. Instead of the 30 to 35 parts per million of sulfur dioxide called for in the still cidermaking process, add 15 to 20 parts per million. Then rack as described. With less sulfur dioxide present, the cider is more susceptible to malolactic fermentation. To reduce the chances of this, store the cider at cool temperatures after racking.

CIDERMAKING TIP

Equipment and Ingredients for *Méthode Champenoise*

- 5 gallons (19 L) fermented cider, with reduced sulfur dioxide
- Cane sugar
- Plastic tubing
- Sparkling wine or Champagne yeast
- Sparkling wine bottles
- Crown caps and capper
- Crate
- Four 2' × 4' (0.6 × 1.2 m) pieces of wood
- Bottle opener
- Safety goggles and gloves
- Dry cider, as needed
- Notebook

Bottling

Before bottling, however, the cider should be warmed to 50°F (10°C). Collect the necessary equipment and ingredients for beginning secondary fermentation and bottling the cider: plastic tubing for siphoning, cane sugar, sparkling wine yeast, sparkling wine bottles, and crown caps and a capper.

Begin by calculating the amount of yeast and sugar to add to the carboy of cider. Most sparkling cider has less sparkle than sparkling wines. Different sugar levels produce different levels of pressure, which is why starting with a fully dry cider is essential. Otherwise, the sugar calculations will be incorrect and the pressure could be dangerously high. Champagne makers often add about 12 grams of sugar per 750-milliliter bottle. At Eve's Cidery, cidermakers add 9.75 to 10.5 grams per bottle. Home cidermakers can choose their preferred style within an 8 to 12 gram range. For those without a gram scale, 2 teaspoons of cane sugar per bottle is recommended. (This will be about 8 to 10 grams of sugar, producing a safe amount of pressure.) Be very precise with your measurements to avoid over pressurizing.

Once you have measured the proper amount of sugar, use the plastic tubing to siphon off a small amount of cider. Dissolve the sugar in this cider and return the sugar-cider mixture to the carboy.

The sugar is food for the yeast, which is added next. Choose a neutral sparkling wine or Champagne yeast, which can withstand the pressure and higher alcohol levels of an in-bottle fermentation. Follow the directions on the package to measure and hydrate the yeast before adding it to the carboy.

Bottle immediately into bottles designed for sparkling wine. (Do not use thinner glass, such as the glass used for beer bottles, which is likely to shatter from the pressure produced during fermentation.) Add a crown cap to each bottle.

After you begin the secondary fermentation, always wear gloves and safety goggles when handling the bottles, to prevent injury from shattered glass.

You should store the bottles in a cool place through the secondary fermentation, which will take a least a month. At 50°F (10°C), the fermentation progresses slowly, which is desirable. A slower fermentation produces finer bubbles. A warmer, faster fermentation will produce coarser bubbles.

Riddling

Through the fermentation process, you will "riddle" the bottles, turning them and reorienting them to slowly collect the dying yeast in the neck of the bottle. The bottles will begin the process horizontally and slowly move to a vertical position. This can be easily accomplished with a crate and some pieces of wood. Fill the crate with the bottles, neck down, and then prop the crate with a pile of four 2' × 4' (0.6 × 1.2 cm) pieces of wood under one side of the crate until the bottles are almost horizontal. Each week, give

Timeline for *Méthode Champenoise*

In Advance

- Ferment a 5-gallon (19 L) carboy of cider, following the process in chapter 5
- Purchase the necessary equipment and ingredients.

Day 1

- Rack the cider, adding sulfur dioxide.
- Calculate and add the appropriate amounts of sugar and yeast.
- Bottle in sparkling wine bottles with crown caps.
- Place in a cool place on a crate for riddling.

About Day 2 to Week 5

- Each week, riddle the bottles.

About Week 5

- Taste the cider.
- If the in-bottle fermentation is completed, disgorge the bottles.
- Recap the bottles.

each bottle a one-quarter turn and a light tap to dislodge some of the yeast that has collected around the shoulders of the bottle and remove one of the pieces of wood until the crate and the bottles are sitting vertically, upside down.

Many variables affect the length of the fermentation process. Test your cider after about five weeks, when the bottles are sitting vertically, by opening a bottle and using your senses to evaluate it. If it is bubbly and you don't taste any noticeable sweetness, the fermentation is complete.

At this point, you can continue with the process, or allow the remaining bottles of cider to mature. Cider that is finished earlier in the process typically has more fruit flavors and aromas; cider that sits on its lees typically has the creamier mouthfeel and yeasty flavors and aromas associated with Champagne. Cider can sit for months or years. As with the amount of sugar to use, this is a stylistic choice. Eve's Cidery cidermakers prefer fruitier ciders.

Disgorgement

The final step in the *méthode champenoise* process is disgorgement, removing the expired yeast from the neck of the bottle where it collected during riddling. The step is not essential, if you desire the flavor and aromas of lees aging. The home cidermaker can simply store the sparkling cider upright, allowing the sentiment to settle to the bottom, a process called "bottle conditioning" that is common in beer making. The bubbles in the cider will make the liquid hazy, but some cidermakers appreciate this rustic appearance. (If bottle conditioning is your plan, the riddling isn't necessary. Simply store the bottle on its side until the fermentation is complete.)

If you are going to disgorge the cider, begin by collecting the necessary supplies: bottle opener; safety goggles and gloves; dry cider, as needed; and crown caps and a capper. You could also use a Champagne cork and wire hood, but that requires additional specialized equipment. Disgorging makes a mess—especially as you are learning the technique. Work outside or in a garage where the surfaces can easily be washed, and dress accordingly.

In most Champagne production, the necks of the bottles are frozen with dry ice which can make the disgorgement process easier, but the home cider-maker can simply chill the bottles as cool as possible without freezing, keeping the bottles upside down to capture the yeast in the neck. The colder the bottle, the easier the process will be because the cider will fizz less.

In the disgorgement process, the pressure inside the bottle expels the yeast and a small amount of liquid from the bottle as it is opened. At Eve's Cidery, Ezra Sherman can disgorge a bottle with a loss of just 10 or 15 milliliters of liquid. As you are learning the process, you may lose as much as 50 milliliters of the 750-milliliter bottle. Any cider you lose will be replaced with still dry cider (or another neutral liquid, if no cider is available).

Wearing safety goggles and safety gloves, grasp the neck of a chilled bottle, keeping the bottle upside down. Hold the bottle in front of you. With the other hand, grasp the bottle opener. As you quickly turn the bottle right side up, you will open the bottle, allowing the pressure to expel the yeast while keeping most of the liquid in the bottle.

To explain this motion in more detail: If you are right handed, hold the bottle by the neck in your left hand upside down in front of your body. Hold the opener in your right hand and position it on the cap. Now use your left hand to smoothly and quickly swing the neck of the bottle away from you (the base of the bottle will come toward your body), bringing the bottle right side up. When the neck is about halfway through its arc (about vertical), pop the cap with your right hand.

Replace any liquid you lost and then recap the bottles. The cider is now finished. Store it in a cool place until you are ready to drink it.

CIDRE

Yeast is naturally present all around us. That's why many cidermakers start the fermentation process with a dose of sulfur dioxide to remove naturally occurring yeasts before introducing the yeast of their choice to the juice. At E.Z. Orchards in Oregon's Willamette Valley, however, Kevin Zielinski makes cider in a traditional style from Normandy, which relies on spontaneous fermentation from naturally occurring yeast. The result is an aromatic *cidre* with soft effervescence.

French *cidre* is dependent on the quality of the apples or juice used. If you have a relationship with an apple grower, you can ask questions about the available fruit or juice. You are looking for juice made from extremely ripe apples with low levels of nitrogen (low levels of nitrogen are often produced by older trees that are not over-nourished), which provides a better environment for a controlled fermentation. In a high-nitrogen environment, wild yeast will ferment rapidly, which can reduce the desirable fruity flavors and aromas, and the home cidermaker must work to slow the fermentation. At the least, you must start with juice that has not been pasteurized or otherwise treated. These processes are designed to kill the naturally occurring yeast and provide an inhospitable environment for fermentation.

French *cidre* is commonly made with French bittersweets and bittersharps, producing very low-acid ciders. But the home cidermaker without ready access to these traditional fruits can experiment with most moderate- and low-acid, high-tannin apples (with a pH of 3.7 or more). The most attractive *cidre* apples are often small, gnarled fruits from neglected trees.

Begin by measuring the specific gravity of your juice at 60°F (16°C) using a hydrometer. Typically, the initial measurement will be about 1.050. Record this measurement in a notebook, which you will use throughout the process to collect all temperature and specific gravity readings and any additional observations about the process. Then fill a five-gallon (19 L) carboy with the freshly pressed juice, and cork it with a solid bung. Place the carboy in a cold place and allow the juice to settle for several days to a week. Sediment from the juice may collect on the bottom of the carboy. If it collects a half inch (1.3 cm) or more, rack the juice into a second carboy, discarding the sediment. (The sediment would provide additional nutrients for the wild yeast, which could produce an overly rapid fermentation.) Place the remaining half gallon (2 L) of juice in the freezer to top off the carboy later in the process, as needed.

After racking, juice should reach the shoulders of the carboy, leaving ample headspace. If it doesn't, you can thaw and add some of the reserved juice, as needed.

Fermentation

Once you have racked the juice, close the carboy with an airlock and place it in a warmer environment—between 55F° to 60°F (13C° to 16°C)—to begin fermenting. In about five to seven days, you will see evidence of fermentation, with small bubbles forming in the liquid, especially around the shoulders of the carboy. Over the next two to four days, the fermentation will pick up speed, creating a cap of brown bubbles on top of the juice. When the fermentation is moving quickly, the airlock will bubble every three to four seconds. (If you don't see any fermentation after two weeks, there is likely not enough yeast present for spontaneous fermentation. Consider using the juice to produce a different type of cider that calls for a yeast inoculation, as in chapter 5.)

Now that fermentation is underway, place the carboy in a colder environment—38°F to 42°F (3°C to 6°C) to relax the fermentation. Fermentation will slow significantly, with the airlock bubbling about every thirty seconds. This is desirable, as it increases the fruity characteristics of the finished cider. You will also control the fermentation through repeated racking to remove the sediment or nutrients and expired yeast as it collects on the bottom of the carboy.

After a week of fermentation in this cold environment, test the specific gravity of the juice. When testing the specific gravity, it's important to bring the small amount of juice to be tested up to 60°F (16°C) so that the results of each test are comparable. If the specific gravity has fallen to about 1.040, it is time to rack the juice. You can add additional juice, if desired, at this point to reach the shoulders of the carboy. Replace the airlock and return the carboy to the cold environment.

After another week to ten days, test the specific gravity again. At about 1.025, rack the cider again. Do not add additional juice. Replace the airlock and move the carboy to a 50°F to 55°F (10°C to 13°C) environment, to finish the fermentation. At this point, the fermentation process will be moving very slowly, with perhaps minutes between each bubble of the airlock.

Wait ten days to two weeks before testing the specific gravity again. If you have a slow fermentation with a reading of 1.008, you can consider bottling this as a semisweet cider, in which all the fermentable sugar has not been consumed. If the specific gravity is higher, however, bottling is dangerous, as the cider will continue to ferment in the bottle. Too much in-bottle fermentation could create enough pressure to shatter the bottle. (For this reason, do not add unfermented juice to the *cidre* at this point in the process.) Test again periodically until the specific gravity measurement reaches 1.006 to bottle a dry cider. The fermentation will not be complete, as the *cidre* process is designed for continued fermentation in the bottle.

Equipment and Ingredients for *Cidre*

- 5½ gallons (21 L) of the best apple juice you can find
- Thermometer
- Hydrometer, measuring specific gravity
- 100-milliliter graduated cylinder

- Two 5-gallon (19 L) glass carboys
- Solid carboy bung
- Refrigerator
- Plastic tubing, for racking

- Bored carboy bung
- Airlock
- Sparkling wine bottles
- Crown caps and capper

Bottling

Bottle your *cidre* into a bottles designed for sparkling wine, taking care not to draw the lees into the bottles as you siphon the liquid from the carboy. Add a crown cap to each bottle. Sanitation, important in all types of cidermaking, is of particular importance when bottling *cidre*, which is more susceptible to contamination because it does not contain sulfur dioxide. *Cidre* is also susceptible to malolactic fermentation in the bottle, which some cidermakers desire in *cidre* and others dislike. (Without adding sulfur dioxide, which could halt in-bottle fermentation, sanitation and cooler temperatures are the only preventive measures available.)

Place your bottles upright in a 50°F to 55°F (10°C to 13°C) environment, out of direct sunlight. Lees will continue to collect at the bottom of the bottle as fermentation continues, producing bubbles in the *cidre*. After two to three weeks, open a bottle to evaluate the level of carbonation. If there is already a high level of carbonation—the bottle will open with a strong pop and you'll see aggressively streaming bubbles after pouring a glass—return the *cidre* to the carboy to ferment to dryness before rebottling, taking care to limit the cider's exposure to oxygen. If carbonation is present but not overwhelming—a slight hiss when you open the bottle, bubbles collecting at the edge of the liquid—it is progressing as planned. Test again in a

month. The goal now is to have subdued yeast, which continues to change the *cidre* in positive ways.

The process from the start of fermentation to bottling can be two to four months. For many cidermakers, longer is the goal. The slower fermentation often produces more nuanced flavors and aromas and, in the bottle, finer, more integrated bubbles. The slower the fermentation, the easier it is to bottle a semi-sweet cider as well. In the bottle, the fermentation process can also take up to four months (the yeast may remain viable for as long as eighteen months). Typically, the slower the initial fermentation, the slower the in-bottle fermentation.

Timeline for *Cidre*

In Advance

• Purchase the necessary equipment and ingredients.

Day 1

• Purchase the best apple juice you can. Measure the specific gravity.

• Transfer juice to a carboy and place it in the refrigerator.

About Week 1

• Rack the juice into a second carboy.

• Place the carboy with an airlock in a warm place 55°F to 60°F (13°C to 16°C) to begin fermentation.

About Week 2 to Week 3

• Watch for initial signs of fermentation, then signs of rapid fermentation.

• Move the carboy to a colder place 38°F to 42°F (3°C to 6°C) to relax the fermentation.

About Week 4

• Test the specific gravity. If it reads about 1.040, rack the carboy.

• Return the carboy to a cold environment 38°F to 42°F (3°C to 6°C).

About Week 5 to 6

• Test the specific gravity again. If it reads about 1.024, rack the carboy.

• Place the carboy in a warmer environment 50°F to 55°F (10°C to 13°C) to finish fermentation.

About Week 8

• Test the specific gravity again. When it reads 1.006 to 1.008, consider bottling.

• Store bottled *cidre* at 50°F to 55°F (10°C to 13°C) out of direct sunlight for in-bottle fermentation.

About Week 10 to 11

• Open a bottle to evaluate carbonation.

About Week 14 to 15

• Open a bottle to evaluate carbonation.

After Week 15

• Drink the *cidre* or allow it to continue to mature.

ICE CIDER

Ice cider is apple dessert wine, a full-bodied after-dinner drink with a balance of the sweetness and acidity of apples. Ice cider, which originated in the cold climate of Southern Quebec, is also known by the French as *cidre de glace*. Unlike many fermented apple products, ice cider tastes primarily of apples.

At Eden Orchards in West Charleston, Vermont, Eleanor and Albert Leger make delicious Eden Vermont Ice Cider from apples as varied as Empire, McIntosh, Roxbury Russett, and Esopus Spitzenburg. The apples are harvested at the peak of ripeness and kept in cold storage until the temperatures plummet, and then the apples are pressed.

Ice cider is made in the traditional way, picking fully ripe apples, pressing them, and using the freezing temperatures of the cold winter to concentrate the liquid. Over six to eight weeks, the natural fluctuations in outdoor temperatures separate the water from the concentrating apple sugars. The concentrate is then fermented in a process similar to the cidermaking process (as outlined in chapter 5). However, the fermentation process is halted before the cider ferments to dryness, resulting in a sweet-tart ice cider with at least 13 percent residual sugar and 9 to 12 percent alcohol by volume.

Ice cider is typically bottled in 375-milliliter glass bottles; at Eden Orchards,

about eight pounds (3.6 kg) of apples go into each bottle.

The home cidermaker can replicate the Eden Vermont Ice Cider process. If you live in a cold climate, where temperatures regularly drop to 10°F (−12°C) at night, you can make the cider outside. If not, a commercial freezer will serve the same function.

Ice cider production does take more space than other apple fermentations. The process of concentrating the juice can reduce its volume by about 75 percent. Starting with eighteen gallons (68 L) of juice in four five-gallon (19 L) carboys will give you between 4 and 4.5 gallons of ice cider, or 40-to-45 375-milliliter bottles. You can make ice cider in smaller quantities, but the need for frequent testing of the specific gravity during the cidermaking process will use some cider. It's a long process for the eight or ten bottles you would produce starting with a mere 4.5 gallons (17 L) of unconcentrated juice.

The best ice cider is made from a balanced blend of apples. There are few apples that have both the sweetness and the acidity needed to produce a tempting ice cider. (Eden Orchards does make a single-variety Honeycrisp ice cider.) Ice cider does not depend on hard-to-find bittersweet apples common in hard cider production. A blend at Eden Orchards may have less than 5 percent bittersweets. The balance is made up of baking apples for acidity, dessert apples for sweetness, and heirloom apples for aromatics and complexity. The juice is delicious. (As with any cider production, choose a juice without additives.)

Start by tasting your juice to help you decide what the final specific gravity of your ice cider will be. Specific gravity is correlated with alcohol content, and a finished ice cider typically has 9 to 12 percent alcohol by volume. (See chart on page 85.) Eden Vermont Ice Ciders are typically between 10 and 11 percent alcohol by volume; it's a stylistic choice that the cidermakers reach by tasting the original juice. Taste your juice. If it is very sweet, it may make a better 11 or 12 percent alcohol ice cider. If it has some tartness to it, it may make a better 9 or 10 percent alcohol ice cider.

Concentrating the Juice

To begin, fill each of the 5-gallon (19 L) plastic carboys with 4½ gallons (17 L) of juice. Plastic carboys won't shatter as the ice expands and are lighter and easier to work with. Seal each carboy with a solid bung and place the carboys in a very cold environment. If the temperature in your area is regularly dropping to 10°F to 15°F (−12°C to −9°C) at night and isn't rising above 32°F (0°C) during the day, you can place the carboys outside. If the weather isn't cooperating with your cidermaking, use a commercial freezer. Commercial freezers typically maintain a temperature of about 4°F (16°C).

If your juice is outside, the natural fluctuations will freeze and thaw the juice, concentrating it. Store the cider outside for fifteen to eighteen days, depending on weather. If the cider is in a freezer, you will take the juice out of the freezer periodically to achieve this same result. Freeze the juice for five days; then remove it for one day. Return the juice to the freezer for another five days; then remove it for another day. Return the juice to the freezer again for another five days.

As the cider freezes and thaws, water will separate, concentrating the apple's sugars in a syrupy liquid. The water will begin to rise to the top of the carboy, forming a whiter layer of ice; the concentrate, a brownish liquid, will drop to the bottom. This separation will be obvious, but not distinct; don't expect a clean line between the ice and the concentrate.

Separating the Concentrate

After fifteen to eighteen days, it's time to separate the concentrate from the ice. You will build a makeshift stand with a 5-gallon (19 L) bucket and some pieces of wood to create a stand that will hold the plastic carboy upside down over the bucket.

Remove one of the carboys from the freezer and place in the stand. It can take several hours for the concentrate to drop from the ice, so you want to keep the environment you are working in relatively cold. If the ice begins to melt, diluting the concentrate, you can return the

carboy to the freezer until the water has solidified again.

Achieving the proper concentrations of sugar is essential in ice cidermaking. The concentrate should have a specific gravity of 1.155 to 1.165 at this point in the process. Use a thermometer, hydrometer, and a graduated cylinder to measure the temperature of the concentrate and, following the package instructions for the hydrometer, test and record the specific gravity. If it is not in the proper range, return the concentrate to the carboy and continue the freezing and thawing process.

If the specific gravity is between 1.155 and 1.165, repeat the separation process with the remaining carboys. You should have between 4 and 4.5 gallons (15 to 17 L) of concentrate in the bucket. Pour the concentrate into a 5-gallon (19 L) glass carboy for fermentation.

Fermentation

The first step is to warm up the ice-cold concentrate. It's probably about 25°F (−4°C) following separation. Place the carboy in a warm place to bring the temperature up to 55°F to 57°F (13°C to 14°C). You don't have to worry about warming the liquid quickly, but you don't want to leave it sitting around too long once you've reached the proper temperature.

Following the package instructions, hydrate the yeast in a container of

Equipment and Ingredients for Ice Cider

- 18 gallons (68 L) of the best apple juice you can find
- Four 5-gallon (19 L) plastic carboys
- 4 solid bungs
- Commercial freezer, as needed
- One 5-gallon (19 L) plastic pail
- One 5-gallon (19 L) glass carboy

- Pieces of wood, as needed
- Thermometer
- Hydrometer, measuring specific gravity
- 100-milliliter graduated cylinder
- Wine thief
- Campden tablets
- Lalvin BA11 or another basic *saccharomyces cerevisiae* wine yeast

- Airlock
- Refrigerator
- Plastic tubing
- Home brewing filtration system
- Bottles and seals, for bottling

warm water, stirring to combine, and let the mixture stand for twenty minutes to proof. The yeast will be frothing. Then feed the yeast with a small amount of concentrate and allow it to continue to froth for about 10 more minutes. This step makes the yeast stronger and cools the temperature of the yeast mixture. The yeast mixture needs to be within 7 degrees of the concentrate mixture. Add concentrate slowly every 10 minutes until the yeast mixture is in range. This step is known as *atemperating*. Then pour the yeast mixture into the carboy, making sure you get all the yeast into the carboy.

Store the carboy at 57°F to 60°F (14°C to 16°C) during the fermentation. The process of fermentation will look similar to that described in chapter 5. Add a bung and airlock.

In ice cidermaking, it is important to test the specific gravity every couple of days. Using the wine thief, thermometer, hydrometer, and graduated cylinder, measure and record the specific gravity. In the beginning of the process, the specific gravity may drop as much as .006 points per day. Quickly, however, it will slow to a drop of .002 points per day. This is ideal for ice cider fermentation.

If the specific gravity is dropping too quickly, place the carboy in a cold-water bath to slow the fermentation process. If it is dropping too slowly, as can happen near the end of the process, you can speed up the fermentation by placing in the carboy in a place that is 60°F to 65°F (16°C to 18°C).

The process of fermenting ice cider takes an average of 6 weeks, but numerous variables, including temperature, can affect the actual length of fermentation in your carboy. As you near your target specific gravity reading, test the concentrate every day. As

soon as you reach the chosen specific gravity, it's time to halt fermentation.

Halting Fermentation

Ice cider is not fermented to dryness. That means you still have yeast and nutrition for the yeast in your carboy when you have reached the desired specific gravity. For the home cidermaker, the easiest way to halt fermentation is to add sulfur dioxide and shock the yeast with cold temperature. Fully stopping the fermentation is essential to the ice cidermaking process.

Follow the instructions on the package of the Campden tablets to prepare 80 to 100 parts per million of sulfur dioxide and add it to the carboy. Store the carboy in a place with a consistent temperature of 30°F to 45°F (−1°C to 6°C). A refrigerator typically works best. Allow the carboy to sit undisturbed for four days. Dying yeast will settle on the bottom of the container.

After four days carefully rack the ice cider into a clean carboy, leaving the yeast behind. Return the racked ice cider to the refrigerator. After one week, rack the cider again, discarding the yeast, and return it to the refrigerator for a month. After a month, rack the cider for third and final time. The goal is to remove all the yeast from the ice cider.

A home brewing filtration system will ensure that you have accomplished this. After the final racking, run the ice cider through the coarse, medium and fine filters before bottling. (If you don't want to use a filtration system, you run the risk of remaining yeast that will restart the fermentation. Prevent this by storing the ice cider at 30°F to 45°F (–1°C to 6°C) after bottling.)

Finally, bottle and seal the ice cider in 375 milliliter bottles. It can be consumed immediately, but ice cider typically improves as the flavors mellow with maturing. Try your ice cider at six months and again at two years and note the changes. Eden Orchards releases its ice cider after one year, but cidermaker Eleanor Leger prefers it after two years of maturation.

Serve your ice cider at 40°F to 50°F (4°C to 10°C) for the best expression of its aromas and taste.

 CIDERMAKING TIP

Timeline for Ice Cider

In Advance
Purchase the necessary equipment and ingredients.

Day 1
Purchase the best apple juice you can. Taste the juice and determine the goal specific gravity/alcohol by volume.

Transfer juice to carboys and place in a very cold place.

About Day 2 to Week 3
If you are storing the carboys outside, allow the natural temperature fluctuations 10°F to 32°F (–9°C to 0°C) to freeze and thaw the juice. If using a freeze, freeze the juice for 5 days and thaw for one day. Repeat twice more.

About Week 3
After fifteen to eighteen days of freezing and thawing, separate the concentrate from ice and test for proper specific gravity, 1.155 to 1.65. Transfer concentrate to carboy, add yeast, and begin fermentation.

About Week 4 to 10
Test the specific gravity every couple of days to ensure the proper speed of fermentation.

About Week 10
Once you have reached your goal specific gravity, halt fermentation by adding sulfur dioxide and chilling the ice cider. After four days of chilling, rack the ice cider.

About Week 11
Rack the ice cider a second time and continue to chill.

About Week 15
Rack the ice cider a third time. Filter the ice cider with a home brewing filtration system. Bottle ice cider.

Respecting the Apple

In most of this book, the methods suggested for making cider at home are based on how we make Farnum Hill Ciders. Many of our closest colleagues—Diane Flynt at Foggy Ridge in Virginia, Dan Wilson at Slyboro in New York, Mike Beck at Uncle John's in Michigan, and others—take the same basic approach. Their ciders are very different from ours, and from each other, but they're all delicious examples of this general method.

Then there are our colleagues included in this chapter, who use completely different methods of cidermaking that can produce equally delicious results—in the right hands.

All of our early experiments with "natural" fermentations at Farnum Hill were microbial disasters. But Kevin Zielinski, an able apple grower in Salem, Oregon, has figured it out. By a happy combination of cleverness and luck, he has some strain of wild yeast around E.Z. Orchards that ferments reliably, and doesn't seem to mind a little stress. Unlike many of his "natural *cidre*" counterparts, he is careful not to allow the microbes to run the entire show, and to finish his *cidre* cleanly in a bottle. Anything resembling vinegar scares us to death here, but we love the faintly acetic bite of Kevin's *cidre*s, complementing all the dried fruit, forest, animal, and other aromas and flavors he coaxes out of his apples.

We tried *méthode champenoise* here as well. Geysers from bottles and alcoholic heat—we're done with that one too, we think. The only way to get tiny, consistent rising bubbles in a glass is to go through the exacting process of preparing a second fermentation from the results of the first, bottling it, maturing it, riddling the bottles, and disgorging and corking them. Most ciders don't really benefit from that elaborate process, and some actually lose their first appeal. But Autumn Stoscheck and Ezra Sherman at Eve's Cidery show that it can be done brilliantly. Taste Eve's for a bubbly standard—if you can even approximate, in your cider, Eve's concentrated fruit, jam, warm spice, and balanced sweetness and acid, you've done better at *méthode champenoise* than we ever will.

Last: we never used to like ice cider. For our money, most of it is cloyingly sweet, with indifferent acid and some vague reminder of fresh apples. But Eden Ice Cider, made in northern Vermont by Eleanor and Albert Leger, is the nectar of the gods. These ciders are stunningly balanced, with just the right bright acidity to balance their amazing fruity sweetness. Yet their fruit and sweetness and acid aren't the main point—they have some sort of hedonistic gravitas. They're the opposite of cloying—potent, rich, full, and beautifully clean. We adore this stuff.

So, delicious cider is delicious cider, but it can take many forms, and be made in many different ways. But one thing has become clear to many of us cider folks, over the years (including all the colleagues named here): The most delicious ciders in the world, by our lights, are either made by apple growers, or by non-growers who pay profound attention to the apples they use, and their provenance.

Conclusion

In Somerset, Normandy, and the Basque region hundreds of years ago, cidermakers learned from one another. They traded information about which apples and fermentation processes made for the best cider. They experimented with new varieties and methods that are now considered classic and authentic. It was these collaborations that led to the geographic styles often called traditional.

Today's cidermaking community is more geographically diverse, connected by airplanes and the internet, not country back roads, but the same kind of information exchange is improving modern cidermaking. Cider drinkers, for their part, faced with an increasing number of cider options, are discovering that there are many different approaches to cider for many different tastes, much as mass-market beer drinkers discovered during the craft beer boom.

At Poverty Lane Orchards, a knock at the loading dock door of the cider room is as likely to be a neighbor clutching a growler to be filled with one of Farnum Hill Ciders Dooryard batches as it is to be an apple grower or young cidermaker seeking grafting wood or fermentation advice. For the crew behind Farnum Hill Ciders, fostering a community of like-minded cidermakers is nearly as important as making cider itself.

Home cidermakers are a growing community within this cider world and can similarly influence it, asking their local farmers for cider apples, supporting other cidermakers and, simply, sharing a great cider with a friend at the bar.

Already, an increased interest in cidermaking has led to an increase in the cultivation of cider apples. This era of cider is too young to lay claim to a style, but the philosophy shared by the cidermakers in this book—the idea the cider should be an expression of the apples—is taking hold, both among cidermakers and cider drinkers.

There's one piece of advice every would-be cidermaker needs: It's all about the apple. For home cidermakers who have practiced the techniques in this book and want to continue to improve their cidermaking skills, that means seeking out ever-better cider apples and continuing the tradition of cidermaking.

Glossary

Some terms home cidermakers will encounter, as they apply to the cidermaking process:

Acetic fermentation: The process through which alcohol is converted into acetic acid, the distinctive component in vinegar. Acetic fermentation occurs when a strain of acetobacter bacteria is present and the cider is exposed to oxygen and moderate temperatures.

Airlock: A piece of the equipment used during the fermentation process to let carbon dioxide produced by the yeast escape from the carboy while preventing air from entering

Alcohol by Volume (ABV): A standard measure of alcohol in an alcoholic beverage, expressed as a percentage of total volume. Cider typically has an ABV of 5 percent to 12 percent.

Alcoholic fermentation: Process by which yeast converts sugars into alcohol and carbon dioxide

Apple brandy: A spirit distilled from cider, also known as *Calvados*. Apple brandy is distilled twice to 70 to 75 percent alcohol and barrel-aged.

Applejack: Another name for apple brandy or a moonshine produced by freezing and thawing hard cider to concentrate the alcohol

Apple wine: A fruit wine, in which sugar is added to apple juice before fermentation or to support a secondary fermentation to create a light-bodied beverage

Astringency: The drying sensation in the mouth associated with tannins in cider

Bittersharp apples: Cider apples high in both acid and tannins

Bittersweet apples: Cider apples low in acid and high in tannins

Body: The viscosity of a cider

Brix: A scale of measurement used to measure the sugar content of juice

Bung: A stopper used to seal a barrel or carboy; made of rubber, silicon or cork and available in solid and bored versions

Campden tablets: Tablets of potassium metabisulfite used to add sulfur dioxide to cider

Carboy: A jug with rigid sides and a narrow neck and mouth, ideal for fermenting cider

Cornelius keg: A steel cylinder with a removable lid designed to hold a liquid under pressure; ideal for adding carbonation to cider

Cyser: A meadlike drink in which honey is added to apple juice before fermentation

Disgorgement: The final step in the *méthode champenoise* cidermaking process in which expired yeast is removed from the bottle

Drop bright: The process through which sediment falls out of a cider, leaving a clearer liquid

Dry: A term for a cider that has been fully fermented, leaving no residual sugar

Farmhouse: A term originally used to describe the small-batch ciders produced by local farmers

Finish: The aftertaste of a cider

Flavored cider: A drink in which apple juice is fermented with the juice of another fruit, or flavored with additional fruit after fermentation

Hard cider: A drink made from fermented apple juice

Hydrogen sulfide: A sulfur compound that can, in excess, cause the unpleasant aroma of rotten eggs and compost in cider

Hydrometer: An instrument for measuring a cider's specific gravity

Ice cider: A full-bodied after-dinner drink made from fermented apple juice with an 8 to 12 percent alcohol

Keeving: A cidermaking process in which pomace is left unpressed for several days stripping it of nitrogen and other nutrients that yeast need to thrive

Lees: The apple solids and expired yeast that collect on the bottom of a container of cider

Litmus paper: Acid-sensitive strips used to measure pH

Malic acid: The predominate acid in apples

Malolactic fermentation: The process through which lactobacillus and other bacteria convert malic acid to to lactic acid.

Maturation: A process of aging cider

***Méthode champenoise*:** A method of cidermaking using a second, in-bottle fermentation to produce sparkling cider with delicate, persistent bubbles

Mousiness: A cider flaw caused by slow-developing strains of lactobacillus or brettanomyces bacteria. It is most frequently described as the aroma of mouse droppings.

Mouthfeel: The sensation of cider in the mouth

"New England" cider: A 7 to 13 percent alcohol drink, in which sugar, molasses, or maple syrup is added to apple juice before fermentation. Raisins are often also added.

Nose: The aromas of a cider

Oxidation: The effects of exposing cider to oxygen

pH: A measure of the strength of acid in a solution

Pitching: Adding yeast to apple juice

Pomace: The pulp of the apple after it is milled, used for pressing

Pommeau: A blend of apple brandy and sweet cider, aged in oak. About 16 to 18 percent alcohol

Proofing: The process of hydrating and feeding the yeast prior to introducing it in the cidermaking process

Rack: The process of moving cider off its lees during the cidermaking process

Residual sugar: The sugars left in a semisweet ciders made by halting the fermentation before the yeasts convert all of the sugars present to alcohol

Riddle: The process of rotating and reorienting bottles during *méthode champenoise* cider production to collect the lees in the neck

Semi-sweet: A description of a cider with noticeable residual sugar

Sharp apples: Cider apples that are high in acid and low in tannins

Sparkling: A description of a cider with noticeable dissolved carbon dioxide

Specific gravity: The measure of soluble solids in a liquid; used to determine a juice's sugar content

Still: A description of cider with no or very slight effervescence

Sulfur dioxide: An additive that serves as an antimicrobial and antioxidant in cidermaking

Sweet apples: Cider apples that are low in acid and tannins, and add fruit flavors and aromas to cider

Sweet cider: The nonalcoholic fresh-pressed juice of the apple, sold for consumption

Tannin: A substance present in apples that provides the structure, astringency, and bitterness in cider

Volatile acidity: A term used to describe the presence of acetic acid in cider

Wine thief: A ridged, narrow tube with openings at both ends designed for extracting liquid from a container

Yeast: A single-cell fungus that converts sugars to alcohol

Yeast nutrients: An additive that can be used to provide yeast with a hospitable environment for alcoholic fermentation

Resources

Boulton, Roger et al. *Principles and Practices of Wine Making*. Springer, 2012.

Brown, Pete and Bill Bradshaw. *World's Best Ciders: Taste, Tradition and Terroir*. Sterling Epicure, 2013.

Burford, Tom. *Apples of North America: Exceptional Varieties for Gardeners, Growers, and Cooks*. Timber Press, 2013.

Copas, Liz. *A Somerset Pomona: The Cider Apples of Somerset*. Dovecote Press, 2001.

Jolicoeur, Claude. *The New Cider Maker's Handbook: A Comprehensive Guide for Craft Producers*. Chelsea Green Publishing, 2013.

Lea, Andrew. *Craft Cider Making*. Good Life Press, 2011.

Margalit, Yair. *Winery Technology and Operations: A Handbook for Small Wineries*. Wine Appreciation Guild, 1996.

Proulx, Annie and Lew Nichols. *Cider: Making, Using & Enjoying Sweet & Hard Cider*. Storey Publishing, 2003.

Rankine, Bryce. *Making Good Wine: Manual of Winemaking Practice for Australia and New Zealand*. Macmillan, 1995.

Scott Laboratories. *Cider Handbook*. Available at www.scottlab.com

Scott Laboratories. *Fermentation Handbook*. Available at www.scottlab.com

Smith, Clark. *Postmodern Winemaking: Rethinking the Modern Science of an Ancient Craft*. University of California Press, 2013.

Watson, Ben. *Cider Hard & Sweet: History, Traditions and Making Your Own*. The Countryman Press, 2013.

Zoecklein, Bruce W. et al. *Wine Analysis and Production*. CBS Publishers & Distributors, 1997.

The People Behind Farnum Hill Ciders

FAMILY

Stephen Wood has grown apples at Poverty Lane Orchards since his teens. In the 1980s, he planted the first substantial acreage of specialized cider apple varieties in the United States, which necessitated learning to make consistently delicious dry ciders, which necessitated planting more cider apples, and so on. He works on every aspect of apple and cider production, and on cider events and organizations. He also collaborates with new cider orchardists and cidermakers to expand the range of American orchard-based ciders.

Louisa Spencer (Wood) works mostly on explaining and promoting Farnum Hill's ciders through writing, speaking, graphic and package design, and tastings.

Their sons, Harrison Wood and Otis Wood, grew up at the orchard. Each of them jumps in on any work needed, in the fields or the cider room, whenever he is home.

YEAR-ROUND CREW

Brenda Bailey manages the Poverty Lane/Farnum Hill office year-round, runs the retail stand every fall, and keeps everyone in touch with what everyone else is doing every day. She started in 1980 packing apples for wholesale.

Fitzgerald Campbell understands, shows, and teaches how fruit trees need to be pruned and trained; he also runs field crews and does carpentry. He started in 1992 on the seasonal picking crew.

Nicole LeGrand Leibon applies her exceptional nose, palate, and experience to bringing Farnum Hill Ciders from the press all the way to the bottle. She started at Farnum Hill in 2000 after working in brewing, tea, and commercial yeasts.

Jacques Tourville maintains and repairs a menagerie of tractors and machines, does field work year-round, and works in the cider room as needed. From an orchard family, he started at Poverty Lane in 2007.

Corrie Wolosin uses her skills in marketing and sales to move ever more Farnum Hill Ciders off the hill to meet ever more cider aficionados across the states. She started in 2007.

Jeffrey Williams works in the fields and in the cider room, and keeps the Poverty Lane home farm looking civilized in all four seasons. Wanda Lloynds works on cider production most of the year, but also energizes the orchard retail and pick-your-own in the fall. Lucille Rogers works in the orchard retail stand. John Smith and Ryan Bishop work in the cider room and orchards, and they run the cider press.

HARVEST CREW

When orchard work hits peak load, the "normal" workweek goes away. Dozens of different varieties must be picked when they reach their best—not too soon, not too late. As October progresses, freezing nights increasingly threaten to destroy the fruit left on the trees. Every harvest, a crew brings in the fruit, presses cider, packs apples for retail and wholesale, and takes the pressure. Everybody works long, hard hours. Most crucial every year are the people with experience in the orchard: James Gerlack first worked the harvest in 1988; William Crawford, Kenneth Woodhouse, and Vivian Currie in 1992; and Wayne Brown in 2013.

About April White

April White's craving for good food and great stories has taken her from the kitchens of Philadelphia to the goat farms of Tuscany, the paladares of Havana, and the tchouk huts of West Africa. The award-winning food writer penned *Chickens in Five Minutes a Day* with the staff of Murray McMurray Hatchery and *Get Your Goat* with goat farmer Brent Zimmerman. She is also the author of *The Philadelphia Chef's Table* and other cookbooks. See her latest work at aprwhite.com.

Photographer Credits

Robert Alexander/gettyimages.com, 64 (left)

Brenda Bailey Collins, 8; 11 (top); 13; 14; 17; 18; 27; 41; 45; 48-57; 59; 61 (middle & right); 63; 65; 69; 88; 91; 93; 101; 109; 110-115; 131; 140; 143

© gardenpix/alamy.com, 62 (right); 95

© Graham Corney/alamy.com, 77

© Jack Hobnouse/alamy.com, 61 (left); 132

© Jeff Morgan 08/alamy.com, 62 (left); 117

Shutterstock.com, 7; 58; 64 (right); 66; 135; 144; 146

Susan Teare Photography/susanteare.com, 11 (bottom); 12; 19; 28; 33-39; 42; 47; 70; 75; 76; 81; 82; 84-86; 89; 97; 98; 104

Wikipedia, 60

Cover images:

Susan Teare Photography/susanteare.com, top, left; bottom, (middle & right); back jacket, top, (left and right)

Brenda Bailey Collins, top, right; bottom, left; spine; back jacket, middle & bottom

Acknowledgments

When I began this project, I had no doubt that I would find the Farnum Hill Ciders crew to be experienced cidermakers; I was already well acquainted with their delicious ciders. What I couldn't have anticipated was how welcoming and patient they would be with this ever-curious writer. I am grateful to Stephen Wood and the entire crew for their hospitality, their generosity in sharing hard-learned cider knowledge, and their tolerance of every question, even ones that came early in the morning, on weekends, and on holidays.

I'm also indebted to Steve for introducing me to like-minded cider colleagues who share the "apples first" philosophy that drives this book and share Steve's generous nature. Thank you to Autumn Stoscheck, who, with her husband Ezra Sherman, makes *méthode champenoise* cider at Eve's Cidery in the Finger Lakes region of New York; to Kevin Zielinski at E.Z. Orchards in Oregon's Willamette Valley, who makes cider in a traditional style from Normandy; and to Eleanor Leger who, with her husband Albert Leger, makes ice cider at Eden Orchards in West Charleston, Vermont. They all shared their cider experience enthusiastically and without hesitation. I also want to recognize Jocelyn Kuzelka of Panacea Wine Consulting, who offered advice and clarity on the not-at-all small issues of microbiology in cidermaking.

Finally, gratitude to those who turned these cidermakers' lessons into the book you hold in your hands: Clare Pelino of ProLit Literary Consultants, photographer Susan Teare, and the team at Quarry Books.

—*April White*

Index

FURTHER READING FROM QUARTO PUBLISHING GROUP

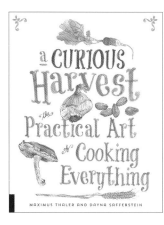
A Curious Harvest
978-1-59253-928-4

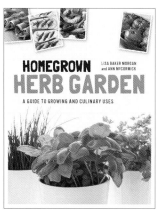
Homegrown Herb Garden
978-1-59253-982-6

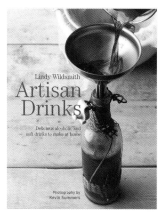
Artisan Drinks
978-1-59253-994-9

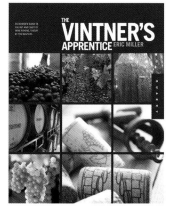
The Vintner's Apprentice
978-1-59253-657-3

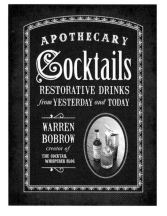
Apothecary Cocktails
978-1-59233-584-8

A First Course in Wine:
Grape to Glass
978-1-93799-413-6

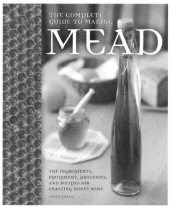
The Complete Guide
to Making Mead
978-076034-564-1

Kitchen Garden Experts
978-071123-496-3

VISIT QBOOKSHOP.COM